INCREDIBLE FACTS FROM RIPLEY'S INDUSTRIOUS RESEARCHERS

For more than half a century, the BELIEVE IT OR NOT! staff has been collecting strange and marvelous oddities from every part of the globe. Amaze yourself with this fascinating collection.

If you cannot find your favorite **Believe It or Not!** POCKET BOOK at your local newsstand, please write to the nearest Ripley's "Believe It or Not!" museum:

175 Jefferson Street,
San Francisco, California 94133

1500 North Wells Street,
Chicago, Illinois 60610

19 San Marco Avenue,
St. Augustine, Florida 32084

The Parkway, Gatlinburg, Tennessee 37738

145 East Elkhorn Avenue,
Estes Park, Colorado 80517

4960 Clifton Hill, Niagara Falls, Canada

Central Promenade, Blackpool,
Lancashire, England

Ripley's—**Believe It or Not!** 15th Series is an original POCKET BOOK edition.

Ripley's Believe It or Not! titles

Ripley's Believe It or Not! 2nd Series
Ripley's Believe It or Not! 3rd Series
Ripley's Believe It or Not! 4th Series
Ripley's Believe It or Not! 5th Series
Ripley's Believe It or Not! 7th Series
Ripley's Believe It or Not! 8th Series
Ripley's Believe It or Not! 9th Series
Ripley's Believe It or Not! 10th Series
Ripley's Believe It or Not! 11th Series
Ripley's Believe It or Not! 12th Series
Ripley's Believe It or Not! 13th Series
Ripley's Believe It or Not! 14th Series
Ripley's Believe It or Not! 15th Series
Ripley's Believe It or Not! 16th Series
Ripley's Believe It or Not! 17th Series
Ripley's Believe It or Not! 18th Series
Ripley's Believe It or Not! 19th Series
Ripley's Believe It or Not! 20th Series
Ripley's Believe It or Not! 21st Series
Ripley's Believe It or Not! 22nd Series
Ripley's Believe It or Not! 23rd Series
Ripley's Believe It or Not! Anniversary Edition
Ripley's Believe It or Not! Book of the Military

Published by POCKET BOOKS

Ripley's Believe It or Not!

15th Series

PUBLISHED BY POCKET BOOKS NEW YORK

RIPLEY'S BELIEVE IT OR NOT!® 15TH SERIES

POCKET BOOK edition published November, 1969

This original POCKET BOOK edition is printed from brand-new plates made from newly set, clear, easy-to-read type.
POCKET BOOK editions are published by
POCKET BOOKS,
a division of Simon & Schuster, Inc.,
A GULF+WESTERN COMPANY
630 Fifth Avenue,
New York, N.Y. 10020.
Trademarks registered in the United States
and other countries.

Standard Book Number: 671-80473-1.
Copyright, ©, 1969, by Ripley Enterprises, Inc. All rights reserved.
Printed in the U.S.A.

"Fifteen Men on the dead man's chest
Yo-ho-ho and a bottle of rum."

In reading this pirates' chantey in Robert Louis Stevenson's *Treasure Island*, we thought it would take a prodigious human chest to accommodate fifteen men. Until one day while sailing in the Caribbean we discovered that "The Dead Man's Chest" was the name of an island shaped like a heaving human chest.

A Londoner named Xavier Edgeworth, who was born on the fifteenth, offered to adopt any foundling abandoned by its mother on the fifteenth of the month. In fifteen years he adopted fifteen of them.

Edouard Garnier, a Frenchman of the time of Louis XV, had fifteen sons serving in the French Army. This alone would entitle him to a place on the BELIEVE IT OR NOT! honor roll. But there is this added fillip that each of the fifteen was the son of a different mother, so that Edouard came by his brood after marrying fifteen women in succession.

We cite this "string of fifteens" both as a sample of and an introduction to *Ripley's Believe It or Not! 15th Series*.

We have lavished a choice selection of BELIEVE IT OR NOT! cartoons on this book. We trust it will captivate, hold, and stimulate your imagination. We can make this claim with considerable aplomb because we have researched every one of the items it contains.

The eminent cartoonist, Paul Frehm, was the art director of this work.

—Norbert Pearlroth
Research Director
BELIEVE IT OR NOT!

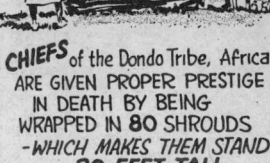

CHIEFS of the Dondo Tribe, Africa, ARE GIVEN PROPER PRESTIGE IN DEATH BY BEING WRAPPED IN **80** SHROUDS —WHICH MAKES THEM STAND **20 FEET TALL**

THE COSTLIEST COSTUME IN ALL HISTORY

COUNT GRIGORII ORLOV WAS GIVEN AS A BIRTHDAY PRESENT FROM EMPRESS CATHERINE II OF RUSSIA A COAT OF SPUN GOLD AND PRECIOUS STONES THAT COST, IN 1762, **$515,000**

THE MARBLE ARCH AT THE ENTRANCE TO Hyde Park, London, **OPENS ITS MAIN GATE ONLY TO THE BRITISH ROYAL FAMILY**

THE SPINETAIL TO DISCOURAGE PREDATORS, BUILDS ITS NEST OF TWIGS WITH LARGE, SHARP THORNS

THE **DOME** of the CHURCH of HAHO, Turkey, HAS RETAINED ITS SOFT-YELLOW TONE FOR 1,000 YEARS BECAUSE THE STONE FOR AN ENTIRE YEAR BEFORE ITS CONSTRUCTION *WAS SOAKED IN MILK*

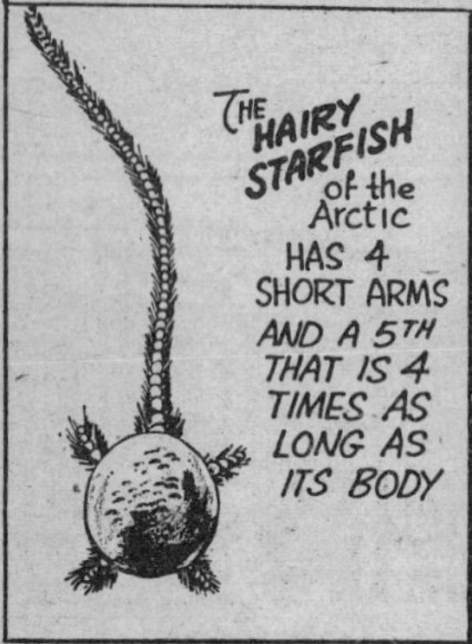

THE **HAIRY STARFISH** of the Arctic HAS 4 SHORT ARMS AND A 5TH THAT IS 4 TIMES AS LONG AS ITS BODY

THE **MONKS** of Mount Athos, Greece, MUST SPEND 8 HOURS EVERY DAY IN PRAYER AND WEAR THEIR LONG HAIR UNDER CAPS — *KNOTTED IN A BUN*

20 **FOWLING** PIECES ARE OFTEN LINKED TOGETHER BY MEXICAN POACHERS TO SLAUGHTER *AN ENTIRE FLOCK OF FEEDING DUCKS*

GLASS AND CUPP SUCCESSIVELY TAUGHT THE SAME CLASS IN METAIRIE GRAMMAR SCHOOL, Metairie, La.

THE MOSQUE OF QALAUN in Cairo WAS BUILT BY SULTAN QALAUN OF EGYPT WHO FELT THAT ITS CONSTRUCTION ATONED FOR *3 DAYS OF MASSACRE AND PILLAGE IN CAIRO*

BOYS on Yule Island, New Guinea, TO MARK THEIR ATTAINMENT OF MANHOOD AT 13 *MUST WEAR 13 TORTOISE-SHELL EARRINGS IN EACH EAR FOR THE REMAINDER OF THEIR LIVES*

EVERY STRANGER ON THE ISLAND OF LIFUKA, in the Tongan Islands, IS GREETED BY WOMEN AND CHILDREN WITH THE PHRASE *"IT IS GOOD TO BE ALIVE"*

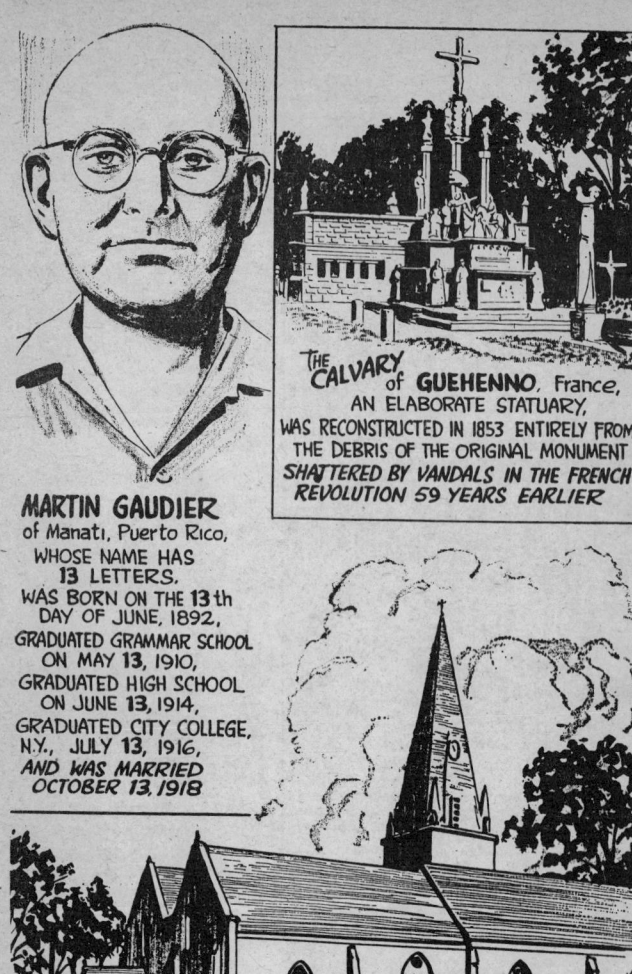

MARTIN GAUDIER of Manati, Puerto Rico, WHOSE NAME HAS **13** LETTERS, WAS BORN ON THE **13**th DAY OF JUNE, 1892, GRADUATED GRAMMAR SCHOOL ON MAY **13**, 1910, GRADUATED HIGH SCHOOL ON JUNE **13**, 1914, GRADUATED CITY COLLEGE, N.Y., JULY **13**, 1916, AND WAS MARRIED OCTOBER **13**, 1918

The **CALVARY** of **GUEHENNO**, France, AN ELABORATE STATUARY, WAS RECONSTRUCTED IN 1853 ENTIRELY FROM THE DEBRIS OF THE ORIGINAL MONUMENT *SHATTERED BY VANDALS IN THE FRENCH REVOLUTION 59 YEARS EARLIER*

The **CHURCH** of **SANTA MARIA** della **SCALA** in Noto, Sicily, WAS BUILT ENTIRELY WITH THE MONEY OBTAINED BY GIROLAMO TERZI, *A MENDICANT WHO BEGGED FROM DOOR TO DOOR FOR 6 YEARS*

A **DR.INKER** SUSPECTED OF TIPPLING TOO MUCH in Trieste in 1905 WAS FORBIDDEN BY LAW TO BE SERVED ANOTHER DRINK UNTIL HE HAD PROVED HIS SOBRIETY BY BALANCING ON HIS LEFT LEG, RESTING HIS RIGHT ELBOW ON HIS RAISED RIGHT KNEE — AND TOUCHING HIS INDEX FINGER TO HIS NOSE

THE **GUARDIAN LION** near Hönningen, Germany NATURAL STONE FORMATION

KING PERSEUS (212-166 B.C.) LAST MONARCH of Macedonia WAS EXECUTED BY THE ROMANS BY BEING FORCED TO GO WITHOUT SLEEP AN ENTIRE YEAR

THE TWO-FACED MOUNTAIN
THE MONK A PEAK IN Goyaz, Brazil, DISPLAYS THE PROFILES OF 2 SLEEPING MEN - *FACING IN OPPOSITE DIRECTIONS*

QUEEN MARGARET de VALOIS (1553-1615) FIRST WIFE OF KING HENRY IV, of France, WORE A CORSET MADE *OF TIN PLATE*

LORD HOLLAND (1773-1840) YEARS BEFORE HIS DEATH SUGGESTED THAT HIS EPITAPH READ: "Here lies Lord Holland drowned to death while sitting in his armchair" WHEN HE DIED THE DEATH CERTIFICATE CITED AS THE CAUSE OF HIS DEMISE "WATER ON THE CHEST"

THE STRANGEST MEMORIAL IN HISTORY
DR. ANTOINE PETIT (1718-1794) celebrated French physician WHOSE FATHER HAD BEEN AN IMPOVERISHED TAILOR INSISTED THAT EVERY HOSPITAL HE HEADED EMPLOY A POOR TAILOR AS ITS JANITOR

THE LYRE BIRD IS A LIAR ITS SONGS AND CRIES ARE IMPERSONATIONS OF THOSE OF OTHER BIRDS

BEGONIA PLANTS in Brazil GROW TO A HEIGHT OF 18 FEET

MANUEL PEREIRA (1614-1667) the Spanish sculptor BECAME BLIND AT THE AGE OF 43 - YET HE CONTINUED TO TURN OUT GREAT SCULPTURES UNTIL THE DAY OF HIS DEATH

AMERICAN INDIANS STALKING DEER OFTEN DISGUISED THEMSELVES *BY DONNING THE SKIN, HEAD AND ANTLERS OF A DEER*

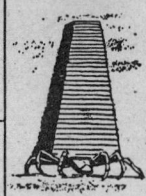

THE **CADDIS WORM** CUTS MINIATURE LOGS FROM TWIGS TO BUILD ITS SHELTER— *BOTH ENDS OF THE "HOUSE" ARE OPEN SO THE WORM CAN WALK —CARRYING ITS SHELTER WITH IT*

KING CHARLES IX (1550-1574) of France ALWAYS HAD PRESENT AT LAVISH COURT PARTIES **10 EXPERT PICKPOCKETS**— IT AMUSED THE MONARCH TO WATCH THEM RELIEVE HIS GUESTS OF THEIR MONEY, JEWELRY-EVEN THEIR SWORDS— *ALL OF WHICH THE PICKPOCKETS WERE ALLOWED TO KEEP*

THE **SAFETY PIN** ONE OF THE MOST USEFUL INVENTIONS, WAS CREATED BY WALTER HUNT, A NEW YORK MECHANIC *BY ACCIDENT*— HE WAS IDLY TWISTING A WIRE WHILE TRYING TO THINK OF SOMETHING THAT WOULD ENABLE HIM TO PAY A DEBT OF $15

THE STRANGEST MEMORIAL IN HISTORY

DR. ANTOINE PETIT (1718-1794) celebrated French physician WHOSE FATHER HAD BEEN AN IMPOVERISHED TAILOR INSISTED THAT EVERY HOSPITAL HE HEADED EMPLOY A POOR TAILOR AS ITS JANITOR

The LYRE BIRD IS A LIAR ITS SONGS AND CRIES ARE IMPERSONATIONS OF THOSE OF OTHER BIRDS

BEGONIA PLANTS in Brazil GROW TO A HEIGHT OF 18 FEET

MANUEL PEREIRA (1614-1667) the Spanish sculptor BECAME BLIND AT THE AGE OF 43 —YET HE CONTINUED TO TURN OUT GREAT SCULPTURES UNTIL THE DAY OF HIS DEATH

AMERICAN INDIANS STALKING DEER OFTEN DISGUISED THEMSELVES *BY DONNING THE SKIN, HEAD AND ANTLERS OF A DEER*

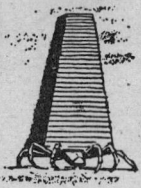

THE CADDIS WORM CUTS MINIATURE LOGS FROM TWIGS TO BUILD ITS SHELTER— *BOTH ENDS OF THE "HOUSE" ARE OPEN SO THE WORM CAN WALK —CARRYING ITS SHELTER WITH IT*

KING CHARLES IX (1550-1574) of France ALWAYS HAD PRESENT AT LAVISH COURT PARTIES **10 EXPERT PICKPOCKETS**— IT AMUSED THE MONARCH TO WATCH THEM RELIEVE HIS GUESTS OF THEIR MONEY, JEWELRY—EVEN THEIR SWORDS— *ALL OF WHICH THE PICKPOCKETS WERE ALLOWED TO KEEP*

THE SAFETY PIN ONE OF THE MOST USEFUL INVENTIONS, WAS CREATED BY WALTER HUNT, A NEW YORK MECHANIC *BY ACCIDENT*— HE WAS IDLY TWISTING A WIRE WHILE TRYING TO THINK OF SOMETHING THAT WOULD ENABLE HIM TO PAY A DEBT OF $15

THE DUEL IN WHICH BOTH MEN LOST "STANDING"

SANDY MONTGOMERY, CHALLENGED TO A DUEL IN DERRY, IRELAND, EXCHANGED SHOTS WITH HIS OPPONENT
—AND EACH SHOT OFF THE OTHER'S COATTAILS

THEY THEN SAT IN CHAIRS FOR THEIR SECOND ROUND —AND BOTH MEN MISSED

THE ISLAND PALACE located on an island in the Thiou River, in Annecy, France, *SUCCESSIVELY SERVED AS THE GUBERNATORIAL MANSION, A MINT, A COURTHOUSE, AN ACCOUNTING OFFICE, A PRISON, AN INSANE ASYLUM, AND IS NOW A MUSEUM*

THE CUTTLEFISH HAS 3 HEARTS

THE ONLY ANCIENT TEMPLE PRESERVED INTACT IN ALL GREECE IS A 2200-YEAR-OLD STRUCTURE ON THE ISLAND OF SANTORIN —*NOW USED AS A CHRISTIAN CHURCH*

Epitaph TO JENNIE WILSON
College Hill Cemetery
Lebanon, Ill.

"SHE WAS MORE TO ME THAN I EXPECTED"

THIS **RING** WAS GIVEN TO THE EARL OF ESSEX BY QUEEN ELIZABETH of England WITH A PLEDGE THAT IT WOULD WIN HIM A PARDON *FOR ANY CRIME* 5 YEARS LATER HE WAS SENTENCED TO DEATH AND HE ASKED THE COUNTESS OF NOTTINGHAM TO CARRY HIS RING TO THE QUEEN — BUT SHE NEVER DELIVERED IT AND THE EARL OF ESSEX *WAS EXECUTED*

THE **CHURCH OF SAINTS SIRO AND LIBERA** in Verona, Italy, WAS BUILT ON THE SEATS OF AN *ANCIENT ROMAN THEATRE*

KING HENRY III (1551-1589) of France WAS SO FOND OF PETS THAT WHENEVER HIS FAVORITE DOG HAD A LITTER *THE MONARCH WOULD CARRY THE PUPPIES FOR DAYS IN A BASKET SLUNG FROM HIS NECK*

16

EMPEROR THEOPHILUS
WHO RULED BYZANTIUM FROM 829 TO 842 ALWAYS RODE WITH 4 SPARE HORSES BECAUSE ON HIS FIRST PUBLIC APPEARANCE A POOR WIDOW CHARGED THE ARMY HAD STOLEN HER STALLION
—AND HE WANTED TO BE ABLE TO REPLACE ANY OTHER HORSE THAT WAS STOLEN

GEORGE L. PERKINS
of Norwich, Conn.,
WAS STILL SERVING AS THE ACTIVE TREASURER OF THE NORWICH AND WORCESTER RAILROAD *AT THE AGE OF 100*

The DOWNSTAIRS RIVER
THE GARGOUILLE RIVER in Briançon, France, FLOWS THROUGH THE CENTER OF A BROAD STAIRWAY

DR. JOHN WINSMITH of Spartanburg, S.C., WOUNDED 7 TIMES AT THE AGE OF 68, STARTED THE STUDY OF LAW WHILE CONVALESCING — AND WAS ADMITTED TO PRACTICE ONLY 5 MONTHS AFTER HE WAS SHOT

THE TEMPLE THAT WAS SWALLOWED BY A TREE
THE PEROT TEMPLE on the Island of Java *HAS BEEN COMPLETELY ENMESHED BY THE ROOTS OF A GIANT FIG TREE*

THE STRANGE SAGA OF "THE ELWELL"
THE SHIP LOST HER RUDDER WITHIN SIGHT OF HER HOME PORT OF CAPE ANN, MASS, ON JAN. 1, 1780 — WAS SWEPT OUT TO SEA AND FLOUNDERED HELPLESSLY FOR 6 MONTHS AND 17 DAYS!
ITS CREW EXISTED ON PARCHED COCOA AND INDIAN CORN — AND WITHOUT BREAD OR WATER

A FOSSILIZED STARFISH found in Australia *IS 20,000,000 YEARS OLD*

THE FLYING FISH
ITS FLIGHT
MORE NEARLY RESEMBLES THAT OF AIRCRAFT THAN ANY BIRD'S

THE TOWN IN WHICH EVERY RESIDENT HAD THE RANK OF KNIGHT

ALGHERO, a community in Italy, GAVE KING CHARLES I OF SPAIN SO CORDIAL A RECEPTION THAT HE BESTOWED THE RANK OF KNIGHTHOOD ON ALL ITS MEN, WOMEN AND CHILDREN (Oct. 6, 1541)

THE LUCKIEST FEMALES IN THE WORLD! — GIRLS in Sirmur, India, ALL MARRY BEFORE THEY CAN WALK

"PINOCCHIO"
NATURAL ROCK FORMATION near Calanques, on the island of Corsica

MRS. **MODENA BERRY**
(1850-1942)
FOUNDED BLUE MOUNTAIN COLLEGE, Blue Mountain, Miss., AND WAS A MEMBER OF ITS FACULTY **FOR 61 YEARS**

THE 30 YEARS WAR
ONE OF THE MOST DESTRUCTIVE IN EUROPE'S HISTORY STARTED WHEN REBELS INVADED HRADSHIN CASTLE IN PRAGUE, AND THREW **3** IMPERIAL COMMISSIONERS OUT OF A WINDOW —YET ALL 3 COMMISSIONERS ESCAPED FROM THE **55-FOOT** FALL WITHOUT INJURY

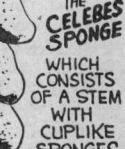

THE **CELEBES SPONGE** WHICH CONSISTS OF A STEM WITH CUPLIKE SPONGES GROWING FROM HALF A DOZEN STALKS IS FOUND IN THE CELEBES SEA AT A *DEPTH OF 3,800 FEET*

THE **COACHWHIP BIRD** of Australia EMITS A SOUND *LIKE THE CRACK OF A WHIP*

THE DRY TOWN
BLIDET AMOR, A VILLAGE IN THE Algerian Sahara
CONSTRUCTED ENTIRELY OF DRIED MUD
WOULD DISSOLVE IN A RAIN

THE COW FIGHTS OF CANAVESE
Italy

STURDY COWS, FIGHTING AS LIGHTWEIGHTS, MIDDLEWEIGHTS AND HEAVYWEIGHTS, MEET ON A MEADOW EACH DECEMBER 1st *IN CONTESTS TO DECIDE THE CHAMPIONS OF THE CANAVESE VALLEY*

HUNTER'S STEW
DR. PATRICK GORHAM of Connemara, Ireland, FIRED ONCE AT A GROUSE AND KILLED THE BIRD, A RABBIT THAT HAD HOPPED INTO THE AIR, AND AN 11-lb. SALMON THAT LEAPED OUT OF THE NEARBY RIVER – *ALL WITH THE SAME SHOT*

JEAN JOUVENET (1644-1717)
LEADING FRENCH PAINTER OF HIS TIME, AFTER PARALYSIS MADE HIS RIGHT HAND USELESS *BECAME EQUALLY ADEPT WITH HIS LEFT HAND*

ALOIS de KRIMPI of La Louvière, Belgium, BEAT HIS DRUM STEADILY FROM 6 A.M. TO 6 P.M. EXCEPT FOR A HALF HOUR REST FOR LUNCHEON — AND MARCHED 55 MILES IN THE 12-HOUR PERIOD

The **WHITEWASH TREE** EUCALYPTUS TERMINALIS of Australia IS ALWAYS COVERED WITH WHITE DUST *WHICH THE ABORIGINES USE TO WHITEN THEIR HEADBANDS*

The **RAREST PLANT IN THE WORLD** A LARGE GNARLED BULB IN THE GARDEN OF CASTLE SCHÖNBRUNN, IN VIENNA, AUSTRIA, WHICH PUTS OUT NEW BLOSSOMS EVERY YEAR, IS THE *ONLY PLANT OF ITS KIND*

A **CEMETERY** on Langwater Farm, in Massachusetts — WITH EACH GRAVE MARKED BY A BRONZE TOMBSTONE — *IS EXCLUSIVELY FOR PRIZE CATTLE*

MAY 6, 1978 WRITTEN IN ANOTHER WAY WILL PROVIDE THESE PROGRESSIVE FIGURES 5-6-78

KING KOBAD of Persia WHO TOOK THE THRONE IN 628 *KILLED HIS FATHER AND ALL 17 OF HIS BROTHERS* HE DIED OF REMORSE AFTER A REIGN OF ONLY 18 MONTHS

THE MONUMENT MADE OF ICE A PYRAMID ERECTED AT Cape Chelyuskin, Siberia, TO HONOR NORWEGIAN EXPLORER ROALD AMUNDSEN *CONSISTS ONLY OF SOLID BLOCKS OF ICE*

THE EGYPTIAN GOOSE FIGHTS OFF PREDATORS *WITH A SPUR CONCEALED BENEATH EACH WING*

CATHERINE DANIELOU 18 YEARS OF AGE of Port Louis, France, DROWNING IN THE SEA NEAR HER HOME *WAS RESCUED AFTER SHE TWICE HAD SUNK TO THE BOTTOM—* SOME SAND FROM THE BOTTOM OF THE SEA WAS CLUTCHED IN HER HAND WHEN SHE WAS REVIVED —AND IN THE SAND WAS A RING SET WITH A 4-CARAT RUBY (1614)

THE "GUINEA PIG" MONUMENT IN FRONT OF THE INSTITUTE OF HYGIENE, in Rostock, Germany, *HONORS ALL THE ANIMALS SACRIFICED IN MEDICAL RESEARCH*

WILLIAM O'MALLEY
IRISH SPORTSMAN AND MEMBER OF PARLIAMENT
ACCORDING TO HIS BIRTH CERTIFICATE ON FILE IN CLIFDEN, IRELAND, *WAS BORN IN 1853 ON FEBRUARY 31*

MOLLY RHOADES
(1767-1853) of Mill River, Mass.,
OUTLIVED 5 HUSBANDS

THE **COMMON SEA URCHIN** WHICH CAN WALK ON ITS SPINES AS WELL AS ITS LEGS *HAS 1,860 LEGS AND 4,000 SPINES*

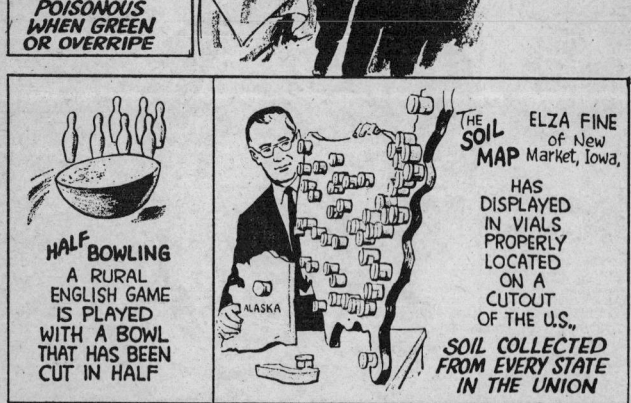

VOLCANIC ROCK Newcastle Range, Australia, THAT LOOKS LIKE A HUGE *RUBBER BALL*

Miss **HARRIET NEILD** WHO TAUGHT ANCIENT HISTORY AT THE MOUNT SCHOOL IN York, England, WAS SUCH AN ADMIRER OF THE ANCIENT GREEKS THAT DURING EACH LECTURE ON THE BATTLE OF THERMOPYLAE *SHE BURST INTO UNCONTROLLABLE WEEPING*

THE AKEE a fruit of S. America IS EDIBLE WHEN IT FIRST RIPENS — YET DEADLY *POISONOUS* WHEN GREEN OR OVERRIPE

HALF BOWLING A RURAL ENGLISH GAME IS PLAYED WITH A BOWL THAT HAS BEEN CUT IN HALF

THE SOIL MAP ELZA FINE of New Market, Iowa, HAS DISPLAYED IN VIALS PROPERLY LOCATED ON A CUTOUT OF THE U.S., *SOIL COLLECTED FROM EVERY STATE IN THE UNION*

AGESILAS AN ATHENIAN GENERAL SENTENCED TO BE BURNED ALIVE FOR ATTEMPTING TO ASSASSINATE PERSIAN EMPEROR XERXES, SHOWED HIS CONTEMPT BY *THRUSTING HIS BARE HAND INTO THE FLAMES OF A BURNING BRAZIER* HIS ACT SO IMPRESSED THE EMPEROR THAT XERXES ORDERED HIM FREED

The **CASTLE OF PRAGSTEIN** in Austria WAS PURCHASED BY DR. VEIT SPINDLER IN 1600 AS A *RESIDENCE FOR HIS VALET*

The **SLOPING ROOFS** of Alpine shelters in the Gressoney Valley of Italy ARE CONSIDERED A SANCTUARY *ON WHICH NO WILDLIFE CAN BE SHOT*

JAKOB IGNATZ HITTORF
(1792-1867)
WHILE A BRICKLAYER'S HELPER IN Cologne, Germany, DESIGNED AND SUPERVISED THE CONSTRUCTION OF *7 BUILDINGS* BEFORE HE WAS *15 YEARS OF AGE*

THE CATHEDRAL OF ST. VULFRAN
IN ABBÉVILLE, FRANCE, BUILT IN 1488 IN THE BED OF THE SOMME RIVER
RESTS ON THOUSANDS OF TREE TRUNKS

THE HAIRSTREAK BUTTERFLY
(Rapala Jarbus)
HAS A PAIR OF FALSE ANTENNAE SPROUTING FROM ITS WINGS SO PREDATORS CAN *NEVER BE SURE IN WHICH DIRECTION IT WILL TAKE OFF*

2 JADE DISKS
MOVABLE ON A CONNECTING RING
CARVED FROM A SINGLE PIECE OF JADE
now in the Ontario Museum, Toronto, Canada

WILLIAM COLLINS (1721-1759)
ONE OF ENGLAND'S MOST NOTED POETS WROTE HIS FAMOUS LINES ONLY WHILE *HE LIVED IN MISERY AND WANT*
THEN HE INHERITED WEALTH FROM AN UNCLE AND DIED AT THE AGE OF 38 IN A MADHOUSE

THE TOMBS of Chiefs of the Afar Tribe, of Dankali, Africa,
WERE ONCE CONSTRUCTED BY PILING BRANCHES IN THE FORM OF A HUT
THE NUMBER OF STONES LINING THE PATH LEADING TO ITS ENTRANCE REVEALED THE NUMBER OF ENEMIES THE CHIEF HAD KILLED WITH HIS OWN HANDS

THE HORNED MAN OF MAHAGAON

DUNDAPPA AJAREKAR of Mahagaon, India, AT THE AGE OF 45 *SPROUTED A HORN FROM THE LEFT SIDE OF HIS HEAD*

"HORATIUS" AN INDIAN ELEPHANT BROUGHT TO CANADA, REFUSED TO GO OUTDOORS UNLESS HE WAS *WEARING A BLANKET COAT, EARLAPS AND OVERSHOES*

SHROUDS in Japan ARE COVERED WITH SACRED WRITINGS AND HAVE ATTACHED TO THEM A SMALL LINEN BAG CONTAINING A COIN *TO PAY THE FERRYMAN FOR THE SOUL'S JOURNEY TO HEAVEN*

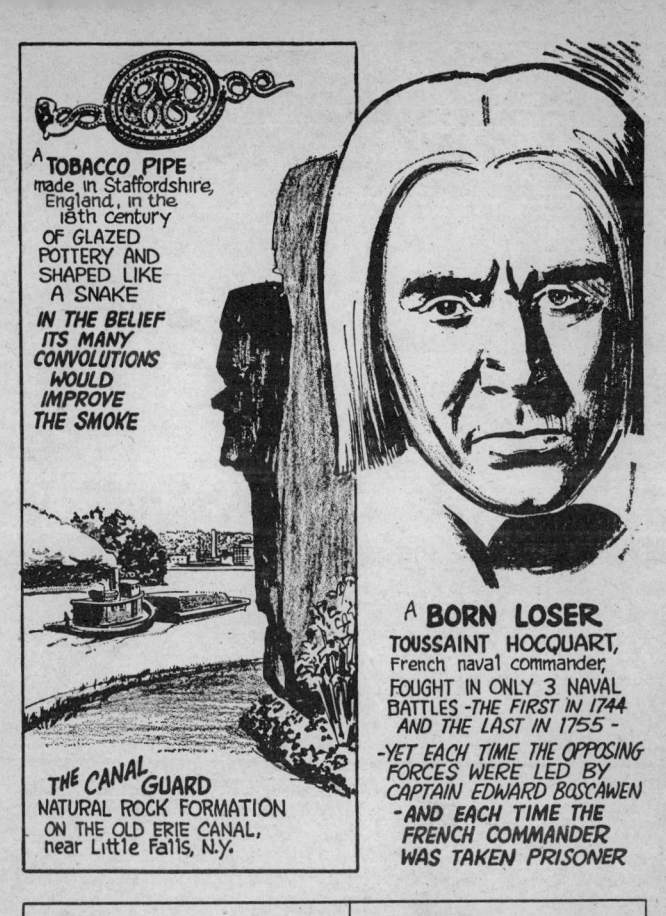

A **TOBACCO PIPE** made in Staffordshire, England, in the 18th century OF GLAZED POTTERY AND SHAPED LIKE A SNAKE *IN THE BELIEF ITS MANY CONVOLUTIONS WOULD IMPROVE THE SMOKE*

THE **CANAL** GUARD NATURAL ROCK FORMATION ON THE OLD ERIE CANAL, near Little Falls, N.Y.

A **BORN LOSER** TOUSSAINT HOCQUART, French naval commander, FOUGHT IN ONLY 3 NAVAL BATTLES —THE FIRST IN 1744 AND THE LAST IN 1755— —YET EACH TIME THE OPPOSING FORCES WERE LED BY CAPTAIN EDWARD BOSCAWEN —AND EACH TIME THE FRENCH COMMANDER WAS TAKEN PRISONER

THE **ABBEY** of **ST. ALBANS** in England IS THE ONLY CHURCH IN THE COUNTRY THAT HAS AS PART OF ITS DECOR *A CARVING OF AN ORCHID*

LEONBERG DOGS A RARE BREED THAT ORIGINATED in Leonberg, Germany *ARE EACH HONORARY CITIZENS OF THE TOWN*

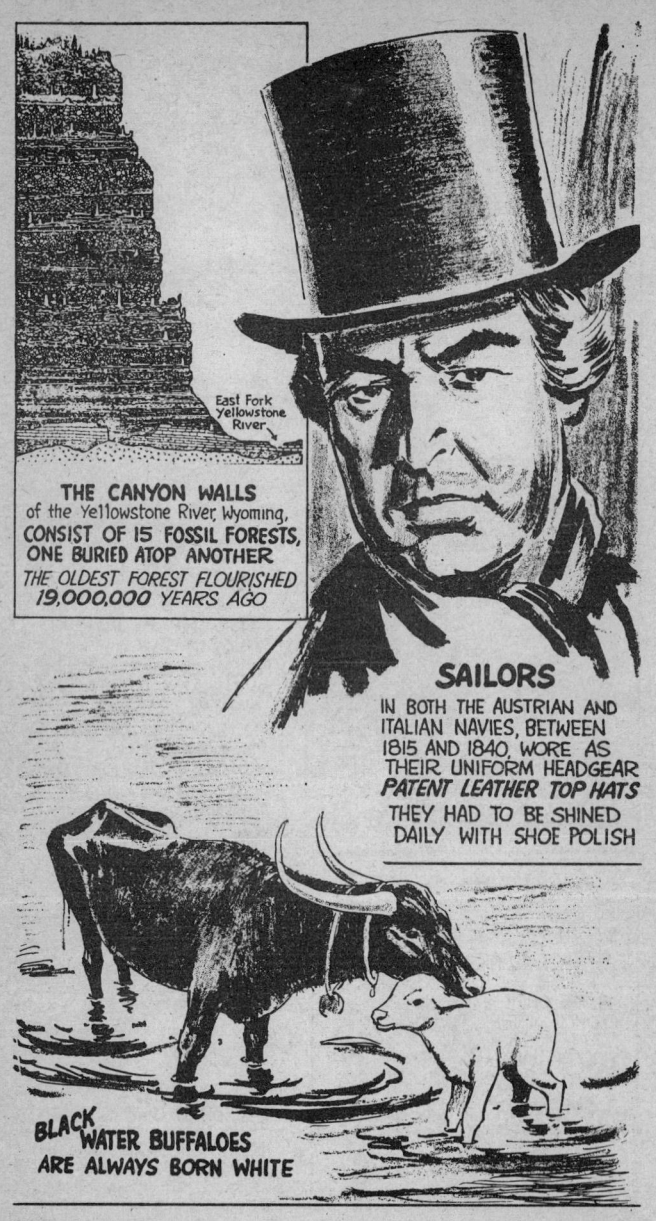

THE CANYON WALLS of the Yellowstone River, Wyoming, **CONSIST OF 15 FOSSIL FORESTS, ONE BURIED ATOP ANOTHER** *THE OLDEST FOREST FLOURISHED 19,000,000 YEARS AGO*

East Fork Yellowstone River

SAILORS
IN BOTH THE AUSTRIAN AND ITALIAN NAVIES, BETWEEN 1815 AND 1840, WORE AS THEIR UNIFORM HEADGEAR *PATENT LEATHER TOP HATS* THEY HAD TO BE SHINED DAILY WITH SHOE POLISH

BLACK WATER BUFFALOES ARE ALWAYS BORN WHITE

THE STRANGE SNOW FUNNELS OF THE HIMALAYAS
HUGE CRATERS LINED WITH IRIDESCENT GREEN ICE HAVE SUCH A HYPNOTIC EFFECT *THAT TRAVELERS FEEL AN URGE TO LEAP INTO THE DAZZLING PIT*

THE FIRST NEWSPAPERWOMAN
MADAME DOUBLET de PERSAN (1677-1771) A WIDOW of Paris, France, NEVER LEFT HER APARTMENT FOR A PERIOD OF 40 YEARS *BUT SHE GAVE DAILY PARTIES AT WHICH EACH GUEST WAS REQUIRED TO GIVE HER A TIDBIT OF NEWS*
SHE THEN PRODUCED A HANDWRITTEN NEWSPAPER - EACH ISSUE OF WHICH WAS WIDELY CIRCULATED FOR MONTHS

THE TOUCAN HAS A FRINGED TONGUE

VOLTERRA a town in Italy WAS SUDDENLY SPLIT INTO A HUGE ABYSS INTO WHICH *AN ENTIRE SECTION OF THE COMMUNITY SLID* (March 9, 1895)

ASAD EXPERIENCE WILSON
1895-1946
HIS MOTHER GAVE HIM THIS NAME

TOMBSTONE in Idlewild Cemetery Hood River, Ore.

THE POET WHO VALUED HIS WORDS ABOVE HIS LIFE

IBN el ABRAR celebrated Arab poet HAVING WRITTEN A DEROGATORY POEM ABOUT A TUNISIAN DIGNITARY WAS GIVEN THE CHOICE OF HAVING THE POEM BURNED PUBLICLY OR BEING BURNED AT THE STAKE HIMSELF—
HE CHOSE DEATH!
January 1260

SIBERIAN HUNTERS USE SLEDS *PULLED BY A TROIKA OF REINDEER*

$2+2=4$
THIS SIMPLE MATHEMATICAL FORMULA
IS DISPLAYED ON THE ELEMENTARY SCHOOL OF Punaauia, Tahiti
—*SIGNIFYING THAT ABILITY TO ADD 2 AND 2 IS THE MINIMUM REQUIREMENT FOR GRADUATING*

THE FILE FISH HAS SKIN SO ROUGH IT WAS USED FOR YEARS AS *AN ABRASIVE*

THE FIRST PICTURE OF AN OIL WELL
A MONK EXTRACTING PETROLEUM FROM A ROCK WAS DEPICTED IN A *LATIN BOOK PUBLISHED IN 1491*
THE FLUID WAS IDENTIFIED AS ROCK OIL

THE INDIAN DUCK RUNNER

WALKS LIKE A MAN

IT HAS AN ERECT CARRIAGE, A RAPID GAIT AND NO WADDLE

HUGHES de PANZIERA of Prato, Italy, WAS ASSASSINATED BY THE TARTARS IN 1312 ALTHOUGH HE WAS SO CONSTANTLY ON GUARD THAT HE *WORE STEEL ARMOR BENEATH HIS CLOTHING THROUGHOUT THE LAST 40 YEARS OF HIS LIFE*

BOAT TRIPS
ARE OFTEN MADE IN THE ARCTIC
OVER THE ICE --
THE MIDNIGHT SUN MELTS THE SNOW ATOP THE ETERNAL ICE AND PEOPLE PADDLE IN THE SWEET-WATER LAKE FORMED BY THE THAW

THE SCULPTURE THAT WAS SENTENCED TO CHURCH
PETER de BEERT A FARMER IN FURNES, BELGIUM, CONVICTED IN 1499 OF DISORDERLY CONDUCT, WAS DIRECTED BY THE COURT TO BE REPRESENTED IN CHURCH HENCEFORTH *BY A SCULPTURE OF HIS HEAD*

ESKIMO ICE CREAM
CALLED "CACPATOK" CONSISTS OF A MIXTURE OF EDIBLE GREENS, SEAL OIL, REINDEER FAT AND SNOW

PROFESSIONAL GAMBLERS
in Germany from 1680 to 1740 WERE REQUIRED TO IDENTIFY THEMSELVES *BY WEARING REPLICAS OF CASH BOXES AND DICE*

THE HOME MUSEUM in Marne, Germany, WAS BUILT ENTIRELY FROM A "KITTY" IN CARD GAMES PLAYED BY A GROUP OF FRIENDS IN THEIR HOMES

A **PARROT** STUFFED AT THE REQUEST OF THE DUCHESS of Richmond -SWEETHEART OF KING CHARLES II of England- IS STILL PRESERVED IN WESTMINSTER ABBEY 265 YEARS LATER

A **SWORD** made in Spain in the 18th century WAS ALSO A DOUBLE-BARRELED PISTOL

GEORGE WASHINGTON WAS THE ONLY AMERICAN SOLDIER WHO SERVED THROUGHOUT THE ENTIRE 8½ YEARS OF THE AMERICAN REVOLUTION *WITHOUT A SINGLE FURLOUGH, LEAVE, OR EVEN A DAY'S REST!*

A STEAMER OWNED BY FRENCH EXPLORER EMIL GENTIL WAS DISMANTLED AT BRAZZAVILLE, IN THE CONGO, AND TRANSPORTED ON THE BACKS OF 2,500 NATIVES TO THE RIVER CHARI, DEEP IN THE JUNGLE -WHERE IT WAS REASSEMBLED AND USED FOR 50 YEARS

MESSAGES ETCHED BY ESKIMOS ON THE JAWBONES OF WHALES

THE CORNER POST OF A HOUSE BUILT IN Invercargill, N.Z., IN 1863, WAS *A LEANING TREE*

GUILLAUME GROU (1698-1774) WEALTHY SHIPBUILDER of Nantes, France, *ANNUALLY FOR 40 YEARS TOOK A $9,750 VACATION* HIS VACATION ALWAYS ENDED ON THE DAY THAT AMOUNT WAS SPENT

A **SHIP LAUNCHING** in medieval times WAS SO HAZARDOUS TO THE MAN WHO KNOCKED AWAY THE LAST PROP *THAT ANY GALLEY SLAVE WHO VOLUNTEERED FOR THE TASK WAS GIVEN HIS FREEDOM - IF HE SURVIVED*

Madame de GENLIS (1746-1830) FRENCH AUTHOR AND EDUCATOR IN A PERIOD OF 51 YEARS WROTE **149 LARGE VOLUMES**

COL. RUTH GOSHON (1837-1889) of Middlebush, N.J., BILLED BY BARNUM AS THE BIGGEST MAN IN THE WORLD WAS 7 FEET 11 INCHES TALL, HAD A 77-INCH WAISTLINE - AND HE WEIGHED 620 POUNDS

THE DRAGON FLY HAS 15,000 LENSES IN EACH EYE

A **BOILED EGG** THE SHELL OF WHICH CRACKED AND EMITTED PART OF THE YOLK —TO RESEMBLE THE NECK AND HEAD OF A CHICKEN

EMMANUEL SCHANTZ of Teugn, Germany, WHO HAD BEEN BROUGHT UP AS A GIRL FOR 18 YEARS VOLUNTEERED IN THE GERMAN ARMY IN WORLD WAR I *AND WAS KILLED FIGHTING IN FRANCE May 9, 1915*

BULLFIGHTS ARE STAGED REGULARLY BY THE MOROS OF JOLO, IN THE PHILIPPINE ISLANDS, BUT THE OWNERS KEEP THE BULLS ON ROPES SO THE *ANIMALS CAN ONLY SNORT AND PAW AT EACH OTHER* THE LOSER IS THE BULL THAT TIRES FIRST —AND THE VALUABLE ANIMALS ARE NEVER HARMED

FRENCH MARSHAL JUNOT (1771-1813) WHILE SERVING AS GOVERNOR OF PORTUGAL, HAVING SURVIVED AN ASSASSINATION ATTEMPT BY A PORTUGUESE PATRIOT, FREED HIS ATTEMPTED KILLER, PAID HIM $20 IN GOLD —AND PROMISED THE SAME TREATMENT TO ANYONE ELSE WHO MIGHT MAKE AN UNSUCCESSFUL EFFORT TO SLAY HIM

RAHMA ibn JABIR

ONE OF THE MOST BLOODTHIRSTY PIRATES OF THE PERSIAN GULF, OVER A PERIOD OF 20 YEARS CHANGED HIS SHIRT ONLY WHEN *IT WAS BLOWN OFF HIS BACK IN BATTLE*

FACING CAPTURE, HE FINALLY BLEW HIMSELF UP BY SETTING FIRE TO THE POWDER MAGAZINE OF THE SHIP

A BUNCH OF BANANAS GROWN AT Burringbar, Australia, **WEIGHING 177 POUNDS**

HENRI MIRANDE
(1877-1958)

A PAINTER AND DESIGNER of Montmartre, Paris, France, LOCKED HIMSELF IN HIS STUDIO IN 1938 AND NEVER LEFT IT UNTIL *HIS DEATH 20 YEARS LATER—*

THOSE WHO LEFT FOOD OUTSIDE HIS DOOR INSISTED HE PAINTED STEADILY - *BUT UPON HIS DEATH NOT A SINGLE PICTURE WAS FOUND IN HIS STUDIO*

WOMEN PILGRIMS ATTENDING THE THAIPUSAM FESTIVAL IN THE BATU CAVE, near Kuala Lumpur, Malaya, PIERCE THEIR CHEEKS AND BODIES WITH LONG SILVER NEEDLES -YET THEY NEVER FEEL PAIN NOR DRAW BLOOD

MALE CUCKOOS ARE 6 TIMES AS NUMEROUS AS FEMALES

THE MAN WHO FOUGHT 7 DUELS -TO AVOID BECOMING A MILLIONAIRE! CHARLES CORNIC-DUCHENE (1731-1809) COMMANDER OF THE FRENCH WARSHIP "PROTÉE", CAPTURED THE INDIAN MERCHANTMAN "AJAX," THEN REFUSED HIS SHARE OF THE BOOTY- $1,000,000 WORTH OF DIAMONDS -THE OTHER 7 OFFICERS OF THE "PROTÉE" CONSIDERED THEIR HONOR IMPUGNED AND CORNIC-DUCHENE FOUGHT AND DEFEATED EACH OF THEM TO ENFORCE HIS REFUSAL TO BECOME A MILLIONAIRE

"THE FEAST OF THE ROSARY" ALBRECHT DÜRER'S FAMED PAINTING MEASURING 6'4" BY 5'3" WAS DELIVERED TO GERMAN EMPEROR RUDOLF II BY 4 MEN WHO CARRIED IT SPREAD ON 4 POLES FROM VENICE, ITALY, TO PRAGUE, BOHEMIA -A DISTANCE OF 500 MILES, INCLUDING A CROSSING OF THE ALPS (1601)

THE PIG-MOUTH MONEY of Siam STANDARD UNITS OF SILVER CURRENCY (14th century)

THE SOLDIER WHO HID BEHIND A WOMAN'S SKIRTS!
WILLIAM GROWMAN, SOUGHT AS A DESERTER IN MICHIGAN DURING THE CIVIL WAR, ESCAPED ARREST BY A PROVOST MARSHAL BY *HIDING UNDER HIS FIANCÉE'S HOOPSKIRT*

A **CAVE** TO WHICH ONLY A FRONT GATE HAS BEEN ADDED IS *THE ONLY HOTEL IN RHOUFI, ALGERIA*

A **SINGLE MILESTONE** in Madrid, Spain, MARKS THE STARTING POINT OF *EVERY SPANISH HIGHWAY*

KING MAHACULI MAHA TISSA of Ceylon TO FULFILL THE BUDDHIST PRECEPT THAT ONE MUST WORK TO HELP THE NEEDY — DISGUISED HIMSELF AS A LABORER AND PLOWED IN *THE RICE FIELDS EVERY DAY OF HIS 14-YEAR REIGN* (77-63 B.C.)

18 BRITISH SOLDIERS
ESCAPING FROM SUMATRA TO CEYLON DURING WORLD WAR II IN A NATIVE JUNK WERE ATTACKED BY JAPANESE PLANES -WHICH PUNCTURED ALMOST EVERY INCH OF THE FRAIL CRAFT WITH MACHINE-GUN BULLETS-
THE 18 SOLDIERS WERE COVERED ONLY BY A ROOF OF BAMBOO SLATS
·YET ALL ESCAPED WITHOUT A SCRATCH

"Belun" an Indonesian word REPRESENTS THE HEIGHT OF DIPLOMACY— *IT MEANS, "YES, BUT NOT NOW"*

THE COAT OF ARMS of Mainz, Germany, CONSISTS OF A CROSS LINKING 2 WHEELS
THE SPOKES OF EACH WHEEL REPRESENTING THE IX MONOGRAM OF CHRIST IN GREEK

U SAW a former Prime Minister of Burma WHO WAS HANGED IN 1948 FOR A POLITICAL ASSASSINATION *WAS THE NEPHEW OF 9 BROTHERS* -ALL OF WHOM WERE SENTENCED TO DEATH FOR MURDER

THE DEDICATED TEACHER

ETTA CURTIS (1858-1940) A TEACHER FOR 62 YEARS, PAID A LARGE SUM TOWARD REBUILDING THE MEMORIAL BUILDING OF GARDNER-WEBB COLLEGE IN BOILING SPRINGS, N.C., WHEN IT WAS DESTROYED BY FIRE A YEAR AFTER HER RETIREMENT— ONLY AFTER HER DEATH 3 YEARS LATER WAS IT DISCOVERED THAT HER GIFT *HAD LEFT HER A PAUPER*

A **LOOKOUT TOWER**
near Pemberton, Western Australia
LOCATED ATOP A LIVING KARRI TREE 200 FEET ABOVE THE GROUND

The **NASSAU GROUPER** (epinephelus striatus) CAN INSTANTLY ALTER ITS STRIPE ARRANGEMENT **8 DIFFERENT WAYS**

DAVID TAUVRY (1669-1701)

HAD A MEDICAL DEGREE FROM THE UNIVERSITY OF ANGERS, FRANCE, AND WAS A CELEBRATED PHYSICIAN *AT THE AGE OF 14*

THE YANKEE DOODLE WELL
Fort Crailo, Rensselaer, N.Y.
THE WELL WAS SO NAMED BECAUSE IN 1758 DR. SHUCKBURG, A BRITISH ARMY PHYSICIAN, COMPOSED YANKEE DOODLE BESIDE IT TO EXPRESS HIS *AMUSEMENT AT THE AWKWARD AMERICAN MILITIAMEN*

JACOB CRANE
of Elizabeth, N.J.,
IN AN ATTEMPT TO ASSURE PERPETUATION OF THE NAME *CHRISTENED THREE OF HIS SONS "OBEDIAH"* THE FIRST DIED IN 1805 AT THE AGE OF 7, THE SECOND IN 1811 AT THE AGE OF 4, AND THE THIRD IN 1812 AS AN INFANT OF 28 DAYS

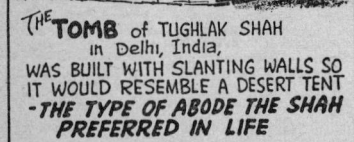

THE TOMB of TUGHLAK SHAH in Delhi, India,
WAS BUILT WITH SLANTING WALLS SO IT WOULD RESEMBLE A DESERT TENT *-THE TYPE OF ABODE THE SHAH PREFERRED IN LIFE*

A BALINESE DRUM
SHAPED LIKE THE TEMPLE IN WHICH IT IS USED

48

A **BRIDGE** OVER THE KERAKA RIVER, in Nigeria, CONSISTS OF 3 TREE TRUNKS —2 OF WHICH ARE STILL ROOTED ON THE SHORES

AZTEC WARRIORS of Mexico FOUGHT IN LEATHER ARMOR SHAPED TO MAKE THEM *LOOK LIKE COYOTES*

AN **EARLY COMPASS** CONSISTED MERELY OF MAGNETIZED METAL —FLOATING IN A JAR OF WATER

A **STONE PYRAMID** in Port Elizabeth, S. Africa, HONORS LADY ELIZABETH DONKIN, WIFE OF THE ACTING GOVERNOR— *SHE NEVER SAW THE CITY*

PAPA DID YOU WIND YOUR WATCH

EPITAPH of CHARLES B. GUNN, A CONDUCTOR, in Evergreen Cemetery, Colorado Springs, Col.

JUSTICE ALLAN ALEXANDER BRADFORD
(1815-1889)
OF THE SUPREME COURT OF THE TERRITORY OF COLORADO
ALWAYS WORE AS HIS JUDICIAL ROBE *A MEXICAN SERAPE*

THE IRON MOUNTAIN
Orinoco Jungles, Venezuela
A HILL OF ALMOST SOLID IRON
-*500,000,000 TONS OF ORE*

FAME IS FLEETING
Xenocrates (396-314 B.C.)
THE GREEK PHILOSOPHER WHO HEADED THE GREEK ACADEMY WAS FETED BY THE ATHENIANS AS "THE GLORY OF GREECE"
-BUT WHEN HE WAS UNABLE TO PAY A TAX IMPOSED ON HIM *HE WAS SOLD AS A SLAVE AT PUBLIC AUCTION*

BLACKBIRDS OFTEN MOVE IN UNINVITED *AND SHARE THE NESTS OF FISH HAWKS*

FRANCOIS HAMEL
(1822-1895)
WAS OFFICIAL EXECUTIONER of the province of Liège, Belgium, FOR **52 YEARS** *WITHOUT PERFORMING A SINGLE EXECUTION*

THE DUCHESS WHO HAD HANDS LIKE HAMMERS

DUCHESS CIMBURGIS WIFE OF DUKE FREDERICK Ⅴ OF AUSTRIA *WAS SO POWERFUL THAT SHE COULD DRIVE NAILS INTO THICK BOARDS WITH HER BARE FIST*

THOSE WHO CARED FOR HIM
WHILE LIVING
WILL KNOW WHOSE BODY
LIES RESTING HERE
TO OTHERS IT DOES NOT MATTER

EPITAPH ON GRAVESTONE BEARING NO NAME
Old North Cemetery, Hartford, Conn.

A **TREE** on the Normandy Road, in France, STRUCK BY CARS MANY TIMES, NOW BEARS A SIGN READING:

ATTENTION, MOTORISTS, MAKE YOUR WILL BEFORE YOU HIT THIS TREE

Automobilistes attention
FAITES VOTRE TESTAMENT
AVANT D'EMBOUTIR cet ARBRE

```
65 X 281 = 18265
65 X 983 = 63895
72 X 936 = 67392
75 X 231 = 17325
78 X 624 = 48672
86 X 251 = 21586
87 X 435 = 37845
```

THE ORIGINAL FIGURES REAPPEAR IN THE RESULTS OF EACH OF THESE MULTIPLICATIONS

HERMANN THE LAME

A MONK IN THE MONASTERY of Reichenau, Germany, BECAME A CELEBRATED ASTRONOMER, MATHEMATICIAN, CLOCKMAKER AND CREATOR OF FINE MUSICAL INSTRUMENTS — *YET HE WAS BORN SO PARALYZED THAT HE COULD NOT MOVE HIS LIPS, COULD NOT WRITE WITH HIS CRIPPLED HANDS, AND COULD BARELY HOBBLE ABOUT*

THOUSANDS OF WINDMILLS

are located on the Lasithi Plain of Crete, Greece
— MANY TIMES MORE THAN IN ALL THE NETHERLANDS

THE JUNGLE LIE DETECTOR
BAFO TRIBESMEN of the Cameroons ACCEPT ANY STATEMENT MADE IN THE PRESENCE OF THIS IDOL — IN THE BELIEF THAT THE FIGURE WILL MOVE IF IT HEARS A LIE

THE MEN WHO WORSHIP PAIN!
THE AISSAUAS of Algeria DRIVE LONG PINS THROUGH THEIR CHEEKS AND NECK *ACTUALLY PIERCING THE ADAM'S APPLE*

"SMOKEY"
A CAT WITH 30 CLAWS

THE OLD BRIDGE of CHATEAULIN France
ONCE HAD 8 HOUSES ON IT SO FOR CENTURIES HUMANS COULD CROSS IT FREE — *BUT ALL ANIMALS HAD TO PAY A TOLL*

THE SPRINGER SPANIEL OWNED BY ELWIN HART HAS ON ITS SIDE THE PERFECT OUTLINE OF *A HEART*
Santa Cruz, Calif.

KING CHARLES VII
(1403-1461) of France

WHOSE DAUGHTER, CHARLOTTE, WAS KILLED BY HER HUSBAND, JACQUES de BRÈZE, *FORGAVE HER MURDERER WHEN HE PAID A FINE OF $180,000*

FRANKENSTEIN'S TOWER
THE BELFRY of ST. ANN'S CHURCH, in Frankenstein, Poland, 125 FEET HIGH, *LEANS 3 FEET OFF LINE*

A REVOLVER
USED BY PARISIAN APACHES ALSO SERVED AS A DAGGER *AND BRASS KNUCKLES*

The NORWAY HADDOCK BEARS LIVE YOUNG

THE ROARING RIVER
THE CLAMOUSE RIVER WHICH ORIGINATES IN A CAVE NEAR Saint-Guilhelm-le-Desert, France, FORCES AIR THROUGH CAVITIES IN BOTH BANKS WITH SUCH FORCE THAT *IT SEEMS TO BE PERPETUALLY HOWLING*

JOSEPH KEBLE (1632-1710) an English lawyer, NEVER TRIED A CASE, BUT FOR A PERIOD OF 49 YEARS HE ATTENDED EVERY TRIAL OF THE COURT OF THE KING'S BENCH in London - *AND COPIED DOWN EVERY JUDGMENT OF THE COURT*

THE ROCK MUSHROOM NATURAL FORMATION OFF ISCHIA ISLAND, Italy

A WHITE FRONTED GOOSE

OWNED BY W.H. LEMBERG, North Platte River, Nebr., LAID HER FIRST EGG AT THE AGE OF 15 AND CONTINUED HATCHING GOSLINGS ANNUALLY UNTIL HER DEATH AT THE AGE OF 45

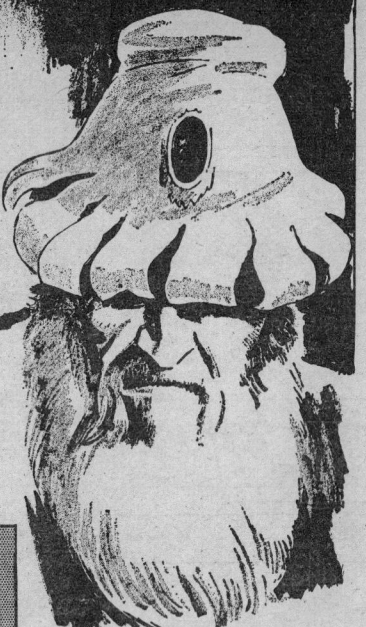

FRANCISCO HUPPAZOLI
(1587-1702) of Casale, Italy,
LIVED 114 YEARS WITHOUT A DAY'S ILLNESS AND HAD 4 CHILDREN BY HIS 5th WIFE - WHOM HE MARRIED AT THE AGE OF 98

The CHURCH OF PORNIC in France
IN DESPERATE FINANCIAL STRAITS BECAUSE FUNDS WERE LACKING FOR A RENOVATION THAT WAS NEARING COMPLETION, FOUND THE MONEY IT NEEDED IN THE FORM OF 100 GOLD PIECES — DISCOVERED IN A TOMB OPENED AS PART OF THE RECONSTRUCTION (1782)

THE BULL-HEADED SCORPION FISH
CAN SEIZE FISH SWIMMING ABOVE IT *BECAUSE IT HAS A VERTICAL MOUTH*

THE GODS of the Papuan natives HAVE CLAY BODIES -TOPPED BY A HUMAN SKULL-

TO PREVENT THE IDOL FROM OBSERVING THEIR ACTIONS THE NATIVES "PUT IT TO SLEEP" BY REMOVING THE SKULL

JEAN du SAINT-VALLIER BECAME SO TERRIFIED AT HIS SENTENCE TO DEATH IN 1524 *THAT HIS HAIR TURNED WHITE OVERNIGHT*-

HIS LIFE WAS SPARED AND 2 YEARS LATER HE WAS RELEASED FROM PRISON -AFTER WHICH HIS HAIR AGAIN TURNED BLACK

THE BASILICA of MOUNT LAVAREDO near Auronzo, Italy, NATURAL STONE FORMATION RESEMBLING A GREAT CATHEDRAL

SKULLS OF DEPARTED RELATIVES IN THE Lake Murray region of New Guinea ARE MADE MORE ATTRACTIVE BY FITTING THEM WITH *LONG BAMBOO NOSES*

AN ANCIENT COFFIN
CONTAINING THE BONES OF A PAGAN DEAD FOR 1,300 YEARS WAS GIVEN A PLACE OF HONOR ON THE WALL OF THE CHURCH OF ST. STEPHEN, IN BELLUNO, ITALY

THE PAGAN, NAMED FLAVIO OSTILIO, ONCE KILLED A BOAR WITH HIS BARE HANDS, AND HIS TITLE OF "UNIQUE MAN"-"BELLUNO" IN ITALIAN - HAD GIVEN THE COMMUNITY ITS NAME

CHARLOTTE CARDINAL
(1799 - 1905)
of Herchies, Belgium,
LIVED IN 3 CENTURIES

"TIPPY" A CAT ALWAYS DRINKS MILK BY DIPPING A PAW IN THE BOWL AND THEN LICKING THE PAW

"LIZ" A WEIMARANER OWNED BY MRS. RALPH COOPER *ADOPTED 9 PIGLETS* Battle Ground, Wash.

THE THRONE of each successive Prime Minister of Dahomey, Africa, *WAS ALWAYS ESPECIALLY CARVED FOR HIM FROM A SINGLE PIECE OF WOOD*

MICHELANGELO CARAVAGGIO
(1569-1609)
ONE OF THE WORLD'S FOREMOST PAINTERS
NEVER HAD A TEACHER —
NEVER STUDIED THE OLD MASTERS —
AND ALWAYS WORKED IN A STUDIO WITH *BLACK WALLS - AT AN EASEL THAT WAS IN TOTAL DARKNESS*

THE VERTICAL FARM
THE ENTIRE BERNARD FARM in Plautus, France, *IS LOCATED IN ONE 5-STORY BUILDING*
THE GROUND FLOOR IS THE STABLE, AN OVEN FOR BAKING BREAD OCCUPIES THE SECOND FLOOR; THE HAYLOFT AND SHEEP'S CRIB ARE ON THE THIRD, THE FOURTH IS THE GRAIN BARN, AND ON THE FIFTH FLOOR IS A BEEHIVE

A **LUCKY CHARM** PLACED BY CHINESE SHOPKEEPERS AT THE BOTTOM OF THEIR CASH BOXES, CARRIES AN INSCRIPTION PREDICTING THAT *EACH COIN WILL MULTIPLY IN VALUE 10,000 TIMES*

59

THE ELECTION IN WHICH THE WINNING CANDIDATE WAS BEATEN

THE VICTOR IN ELECTIONS IN THE New Hebrides islands *WAS SELECTED BY VOTERS WIELDING CLUBS*

THE ELECTIVE OFFICE WAS GIVEN TO THE CANDIDATE WHO WITHSTOOD THE BEATING BEST

AN ENSIGN
THE LOWEST COMMISSIONED RANK IN THE ROYAL MUSKETEERS OF FRANCE ACHIEVED HIS COMMISSION IN THE 17th CENTURY *BY PAYING THE EQUIVALENT OF $39,000*

THE ELF OWL
WILL NEST ONLY IN A HOLE MADE BY A WOODPECKER IN THE TRUNK OF A CACTUS

A PARROT and a CAT
WERE TRAINED BY MARY NOON, of Cambridge, Mass., *TO EAT FROM THE SAME DISH*

DR. FERDINAND SAUERBRUCH

(1875-1951) CELEBRATED GERMAN SURGEON, ONCE FAILED 6 CANDIDATES FOR A MEDICAL DEGREE IN ZURICH, SWITZERLAND, BECAUSE THEY FAILED TO PROPERLY ANSWER THIS QUESTION:
"WHY DOES MY DOG WAG ITS TAIL?"
THE PROPER ANSWER: *"BECAUSE IT IS HAPPY TO SEE US!"* (1911)

TOKEN COINS

WITH A FACE VALUE OF ONE DOLLAR, ISSUED BY THE SWEDISH GOVERNMENT IN 1715, PROVED SO UNPOPULAR THAT THEY WERE REISSUED —OFFICIALLY VALUED AT ¼ OF A CENT

CANDELABRA SPRUCE near Neuchatel, Switzerland

THE MAN WHO OUTWRESTLED A CROCODILE!

SAMUEL POOTCHEMUNKA, an aborigine of the York Peninsula, Australia, WITH ONLY *HIS BARE HANDS* SAVED *HIS DAUGHTER-IN-LAW* FROM A CROCODILE THAT HAD PULLED HER INTO THE WATER FROM A DUGOUT CANOE (OCT., 1952)

MOHAMMEDAN WOMEN UNWILLING TO EXPOSE EVEN THEIR EYES, WEAR VEILS WITH THE EYEPIECE MASKED BY WIRE MESH

THE "ANTARCHITECTS" THE NEST of the GARDEN ANT IS CONSTRUCTED BY HOLLOWING OUT THE SOIL TO FORM MANY CHAMBERS—

THE PARTITIONS ARE REINFORCED BY "BEAMS" MADE OF GRASS AND PLANT STEMS

POSTER IN THE PRESIDENTIAL CAMPAIGN OF 1880 PREDICTING ELECTION OF JAMES GARFIELD— WITH THE CIGAR, THE LINE READS: "YOU WILL SEE GAR-FIELD ELECTED"

YOU CAN BET YOUR LIFE, YOU WILL.
FIELD ELECTED

THE MOST EXPERT SPEAR THROWERS IN THE WORLD
THE MANDAN INDIANS of North Dakota REGULARLY PLAYED A GAME IN WHICH A LONG SPEAR WAS HURLED THROUGH A SMALL WOODEN RING AS IT ROLLED PAST ON THE GROUND

A **MONUMENT** THAT STANDS IN 3 COUNTRIES – FINLAND – NORWAY AND SWEDEN

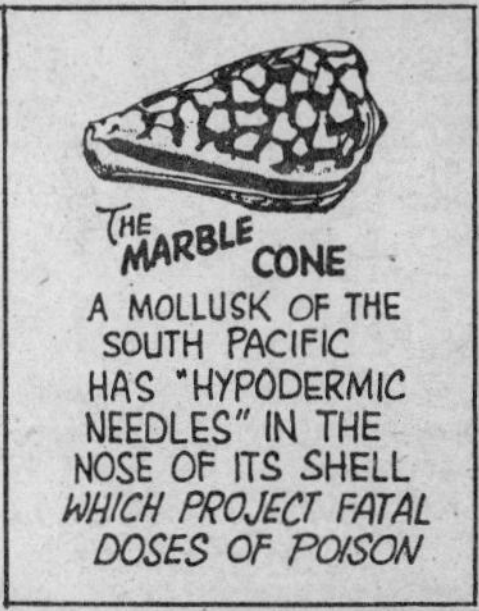

THE **MARBLE** CONE
A MOLLUSK OF THE SOUTH PACIFIC HAS "HYPODERMIC NEEDLES" IN THE NOSE OF ITS SHELL *WHICH PROJECT FATAL DOSES OF POISON*

A **WOMAN** of the Kuanyama Tribe of Ovamboland, Africa, WEARS A BAR LINKING THE TWO REAR HORNS OF HER HEADDRESS *TO ANNOUNCE THAT SHE IS* **A REMARRIED DIVORCEE**

THE GULF OF MORBIHAN in Brittany, France, IS STUDDED WITH 365 ISLANDS – *ONE FOR EACH DAY OF THE YEAR*

COUNTESS de POLIGNAC AND THE MARQUISE de NESLE
2 FRENCH NOBLEWOMEN, IN A DISPUTE OVER THE AFFECTIONS OF THE DUKE de RICHELIEU *FOUGHT A PISTOL DUEL AT 25 PACES —* MADAME de NESLE WAS WOUNDED IN THE SHOULDER.
Paris, France - Sept. 10, 1718

THE TOWER of St. Michele Church, in Prignano, Italy, IS PRESERVED AS A MEMORIAL TO VETERANS OF WORLD WAR I *ALTHOUGH THE CHURCH ITSELF WAS DEMOLISHED*

Children of the Bassari Tribe of Togo, Africa, ARE PLACED ON MATS IN THEIR HUTS BENEATH BOWLS, *EACH CONTAINING THE FAVORITE FOOD OF AN ANCESTOR* THE FOOD THE CHILD FIRST REACHES FOR DETERMINES THE ANCESTOR WHOSE NAME THE CHILD WILL BEAR

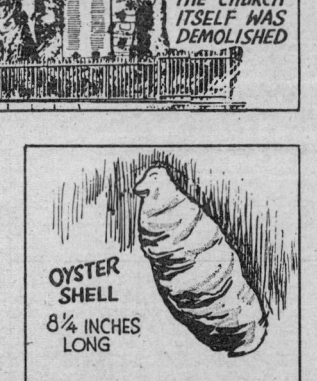

OYSTER SHELL 8¼ INCHES LONG

A BLOSSOM FORMED OF SAND BARITE CRYSTALS -FOUND IN OKLAHOMA

LT. COL. VILLOT DE LA TOUR of the French Army, WAS APPOINTED A GENERAL ON MAY 15, 1793, BUT BECAUSE OF AN ERROR HE CONTINUED TO SERVE AS A LT. COLONEL *FOR 18 YEARS*

GLACIER FLEA (isotoma saltans) IS THE ONLY CREATURE IN NATURE THAT SPENDS ITS ENTIRE LIFE UPON *ICE AND SNOW*

BONDO GIRLS of India RAKE UP DEBRIS WITH A CHILD *SQUATTING ON THE RAKE*

OTOMI INDIANS of Puebla, Mexico, ARE CURED OF VERTIGO BY CLIMBING TO THE TOP OF A HUGE POLE DURING FEAST DAYS AND PERFORMING A RITUAL DANCE **90 FEET IN THE AIR**

REV. DAVID WILLIAMSON (1634-1706) of Edinburgh, Scotland, WAS MARRIED **7** TIMES —HAVING BURIED **6** WIVES

THE FANTAILED FLATTERER THE BLACK AND WHITE FANTAIL of Australia CONSTANTLY CALLS OUT *"SWEET PRETTY CREATURE"*

HINDU HOLY MEN OFTEN TRAIN FOR THEIR AUSTERITIES BY SITTING FOR HOURS ON A SWING *STUDDED WITH NAILS*

MARCUS FIRMUS
A MERCHANT OF Seleucia, Syria, WHO PROCLAIMED HIMSELF EMPEROR OF EGYPT IN 271 OFTEN CONSUMED IN A SINGLE DAY A *300-POUND OSTRICH*

THE **BOATS** used by Kotoko fishermen of Africa *ARE MADE OF FLAT BOARDS-SEWN TOGETHER-* NOT A SINGLE NAIL IS USED-BUT STRAW STUFFED INTO THE CREVICES SWELLS TO MAKE THE BOATS WATERPROOF

THE **HARLEQUIN BEETLE** of South America HAS FRONT LEGS 3 TIMES AS LONG AS ITS BODY, AND ANTENNAE TWICE AS LONG AS ITS BODY

THE CHISEL CANT HELP HER ANY

EPITAPH ON THE GRAVESTONE OF ASENATH SOULE WHO DIED AT THE AGE OF 87 Mayflower Cemetery, Duxbury, Mass.

The SIGNATURE of EMPEROR OTTO I, of Germany, WAS A STRAIGHT LINE
THE ROYAL MONOGRAM WAS DRAWN BY A SCRIBE AND THE EMPEROR MERELY ADDED A HORIZONTAL LINE THROUGH ITS CENTER

CAPTAIN STEPHEN MARTIN
(1665-1740)
AT THE OCCASION OF A FORMAL BALL IN 1708, WAS FOUND TO BE THE ONLY ONE OF 2,000 OFFICERS OF THE ROYAL BRITISH NAVY WHO KNEW HOW TO DANCE

THOMAS and PIERRE CORNEILLE
BROTHERS WHO BECAME NOTED FRENCH DRAMATISTS
EACH WROTE 42 PLAYS
AND BECAUSE THOMAS WAS EXACTLY 19 YEARS AND 2 MONTHS YOUNGER THAN PIERRE, THEY MARRIED 2 SISTERS, MARIE AND MARGUERITE
— WHO HAD EXACTLY THE SAME AGE DIFFERENCE AS THEIR HUSBANDS

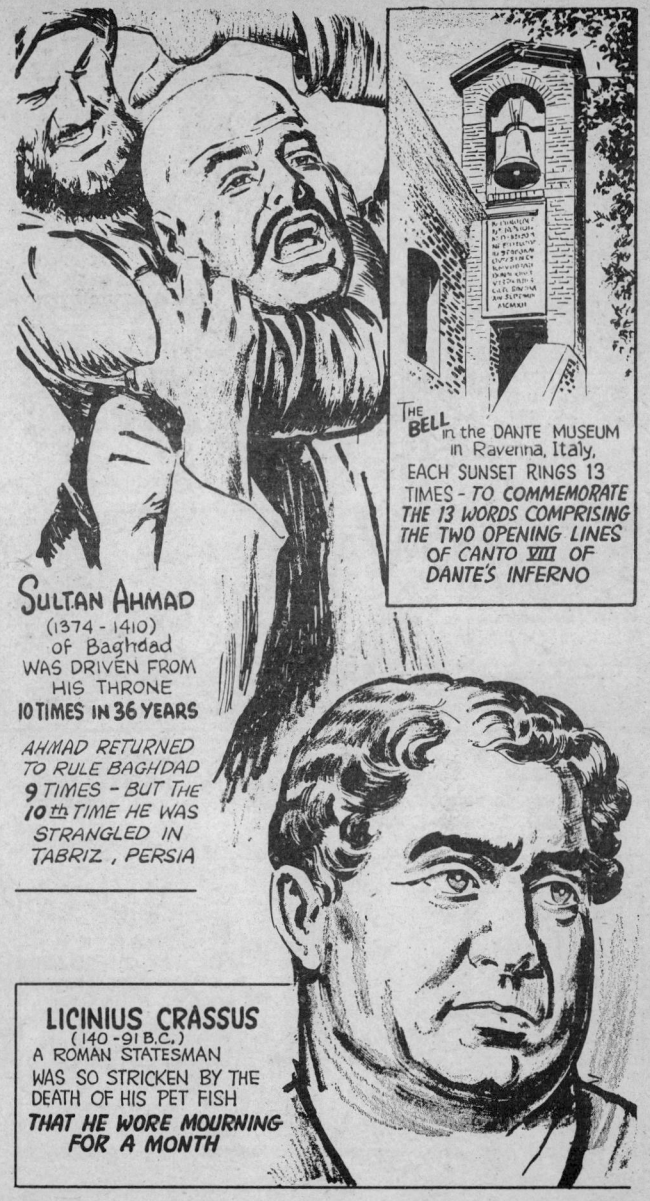

The BELL in the DANTE MUSEUM in Ravenna, Italy, EACH SUNSET RINGS 13 TIMES - TO COMMEMORATE THE 13 WORDS COMPRISING THE TWO OPENING LINES OF CANTO VIII OF DANTE'S INFERNO

SULTAN AHMAD
(1374 - 1410)
of Baghdad
WAS DRIVEN FROM HIS THRONE
10 TIMES IN 36 YEARS

*AHMAD RETURNED TO RULE BAGHDAD **9 TIMES** - BUT THE **10th** TIME HE WAS STRANGLED IN TABRIZ, PERSIA*

LICINIUS CRASSUS
(140 - 91 B.C.)
A ROMAN STATESMAN
WAS SO STRICKEN BY THE DEATH OF HIS PET FISH
THAT HE WORE MOURNING FOR A MONTH

69

THE MASKED CRAB HAS A SHELL RESEMBLING A HUMAN MASK

MARSHAL JEAN-BAPTISTE de BESSIÈRES (1769-1813)

WAS THE ONLY FRENCH SOLDIER WHO DARED DEFY NAPOLEON'S EDICT THAT EVERY MEMBER OF HIS ARMY *HAVE A HAIRCUT*

THE **RAFTS** CONSTRUCTED BY NATIVES OF KASHMIR ARE KEPT AFLOAT BY GOATSKINS — THE SKIN OF ONE LEG IS LEFT UNSTITCHED SO THE SKINS CAN BE INFLATED BY BLOWING THROUGH THE LEG

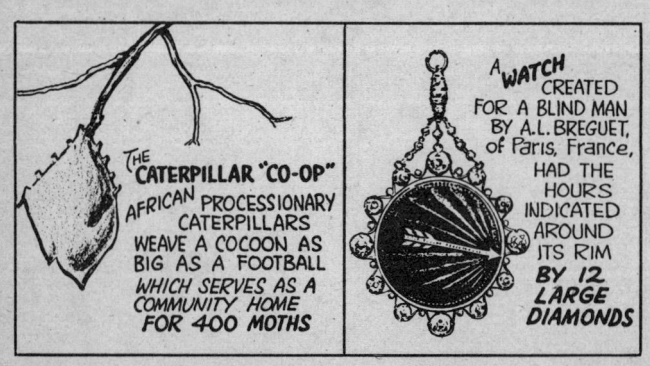

THE **CATERPILLAR "CO-OP"**
AFRICAN PROCESSIONARY CATERPILLARS WEAVE A COCOON AS BIG AS A FOOTBALL WHICH SERVES AS A COMMUNITY HOME FOR 400 MOTHS

A **WATCH** CREATED FOR A BLIND MAN BY A.L. BREGUET, of Paris, France, HAD THE HOURS INDICATED AROUND ITS RIM *BY 12 LARGE DIAMONDS*

MOUNT TESTACCIO in Rome
164 FEET HIGH
CONSISTS OF BROKEN POTTERY JARS
AMASSED OVER A PERIOD OF **600** YEARS—
THEY WERE DISCARDED BY AN OLD ROMAN
MARKET—WHICH RECEIVED ALL ITS
FOOD SUPPLIES IN TERRA-COTTA JARS

THE **CHURCH of SANTA MARIA MAGGIORE** in Sipontum, Italy,
STILL HOLDS SERVICES REGULARLY ALTHOUGH
EVERY OTHER BUILDING IN THE
COMMUNITY HAS CRUMBLED TO DUST SINCE
THE TOWN WAS ABANDONED 711 YEARS AGO

The STEEL MINISKIRT
KING HENRY VIII of England
OFTEN WORE A COAT OF ARMS
WITH A PLEATED MINISKIRT
THE SKIRT LOOKED LIKE CLOTH AND WAS
EQUIPPED WITH HINGES SO IT COULD BE
RAISED STILL HIGHER WHEN THE
MONARCH WAS ON HORSEBACK

EMPEROR AUGUSTUS CAESAR (63 B.C.-14 A.D.) WAS THE ONLY ROMAN MONARCH WHO LIVED LONG ENOUGH TO SEE HIS *GREAT-GREAT GRANDSON*

A DOUBLE MIRAGE SEEN ON VERY HOT DAYS near Kufra, in the Sahara Desert, TAKES THE FORM OF AN OASIS, WITH PALM TREES AND A LAKE -*WITH AN INVERTED REFLECTION IN THE SKY*

ADMIRAL SIR ALGERNON HENEAGE (1834-1915) TOO FINICKY TO HAVE HIS SHIRTS LAUNDERED ABOARD SHIP, ALWAYS SAILED WITH 270 SHIRTS SO HE COULD WEAR A CLEAN SHIRT THAT HAD BEEN LAUNDERED IN ENGLAND, EVERY DAY *FOR 9 MONTHS*

RURAL BRIDGES
in the Cevennes Mountain
District of France

MUST BE ESPECIALLY BUILT TO WITHSTAND FLOODS BECAUSE THE AREA OFTEN RECORDS *12 INCHES OF RAIN IN 24 HOURS*

THE **GIRAFFE** HAS A TONGUE SO LONG IT USES IT TO CLEAN ITS EARS

VISCOUNT TURENNE
(1611-1675)
A FRENCH FIELD MARSHAL in the Battle of Sassbach on July 27, 1675,
WAS SUFFOCATED BY A CANNONBALL —
THE MISSILE HIT HIM IN THE STOMACH, KNOCKING THE BREATH OUT OF HIM — AND HE DIED OF SUFFOCATION ALTHOUGH HE WAS NOT EVEN SCRATCHED

73

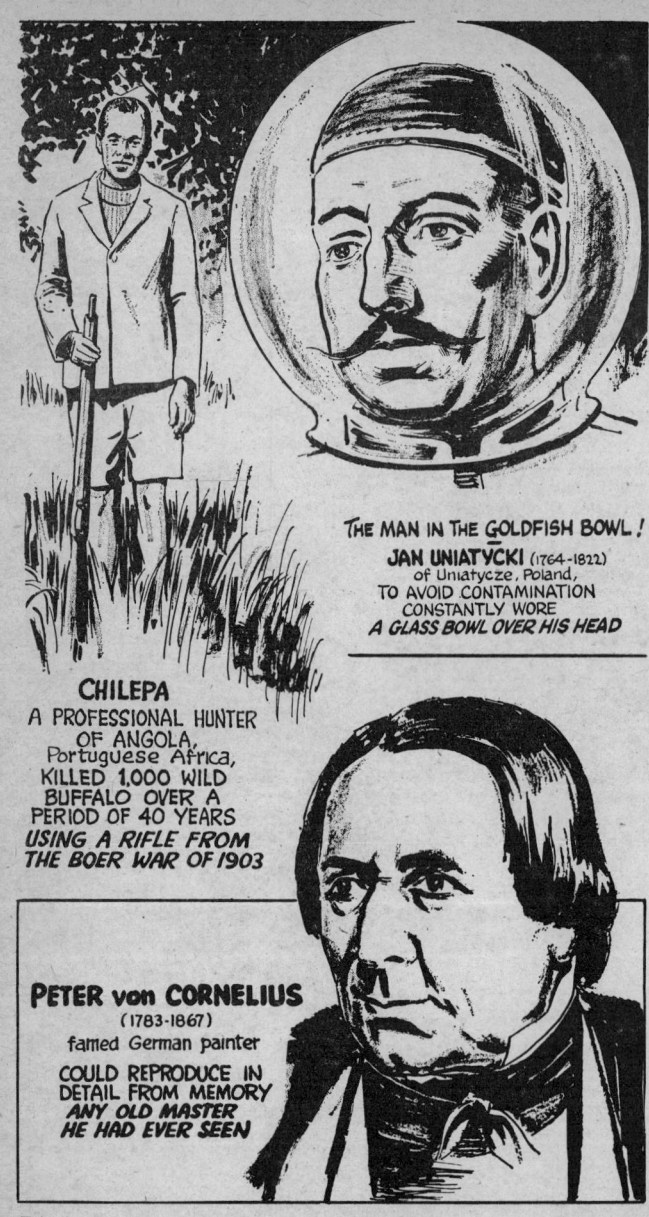

THE MAN IN THE GOLDFISH BOWL!
JAN UNIATYCKI (1764-1822)
of Uniatycze, Poland,
TO AVOID CONTAMINATION
CONSTANTLY WORE
A GLASS BOWL OVER HIS HEAD

CHILEPA
A PROFESSIONAL HUNTER
OF ANGOLA,
Portuguese Africa,
KILLED 1,000 WILD
BUFFALO OVER A
PERIOD OF 40 YEARS
*USING A RIFLE FROM
THE BOER WAR OF 1903*

PETER von CORNELIUS
(1783-1867)
famed German painter

COULD REPRODUCE IN
DETAIL FROM MEMORY
*ANY OLD MASTER
HE HAD EVER SEEN*

GRAND DUCHESS MARIE-ADELAIDE
(1894 - 1924)
WHO GOVERNED THE GRAND DUCHY OF LUXEMBOURG FROM 1912 UNTIL 1919 *WAS THE FIRST NATIVE-BORN RULER OF HER COUNTRY IN 598 YEARS*

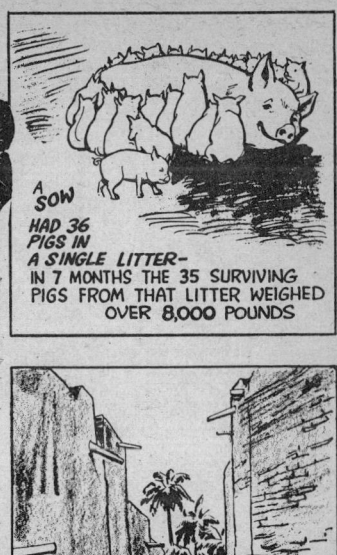

A SOW HAD 36 PIGS IN A *SINGLE LITTER* — IN 7 MONTHS THE 35 SURVIVING PIGS FROM THAT LITTER WEIGHED OVER 8,000 POUNDS

THE UNFRIENDLIEST TOWN EIN DIS a village in the Sahara Desert, Algeria, IS INHABITED ENTIRELY BY MEMBERS OF ONE FAMILY *-AND NO ONE ELSE CAN REST THERE EVEN FOR A SINGLE NIGHT*

A SILVER BATHTUB WAS LISTED ON THE MENU OF the Meot Restaurant, in Paris, France, SO LEADERS OF THE FRENCH REVOLUTION COULD DINE LEISURELY *WHILE TAKING A CHAMPAGNE BATH*

THE BAPTISMAL CHAPEL of the Cathedral of Ischia, Italy, WAS ORIGINALLY AN *ANCIENT COFFIN*

DHAHER BIAMR ALLAH (1173-1226) IN JAIL WHEN HIS FATHER'S DEATH MADE HIM CALIPH OF BAGHDAD *INSISTED UPON SPENDING THE REMAINDER OF THAT NIGHT IN HIS PRISON CELL*

CHILDREN of Penrhyn Island, in the Pacific, PADDLE TO SCHOOL EVERY DAY IN *WOODEN BATHTUBS*

A **COMBINATION SOFA AND BATHTUB** was advertised in Chicago, Illinois, in 1884 *AS A "HOUSEHOLD NECESSITY"*

NATURE'S RAFTS
LAKE LUALABA, A SOURCE OF the Congo River, in Africa, IS COVERED WITH PAPYRUS RAFTS *WHICH FLOAT FROM SHORE TO SHORE*

JEAN JADOT
(1862-1932) AN ENGINEER, HAD 3 BROTHERS WHO WERE GRADUATE ENGINEERS, AS WERE 2 BROTHERS-IN-LAW, 5 UNCLES AND 2 NEPHEWS — AND ALL BUILT RAILROADS IN CHINA AND THE CONGO

RITZ KENT ARTHUR WILLIAM JOHN de RITZ
A Great Dane, ATTENDED Hillsdale College, Mich., DAILY FOR 4 YEARS, AND AS A MEMBER OF THE CLASS OF 1940 WORE A MORTARBOARD AS IT WAS AWARDED THE DEGREES *OF DOCTOR OF DOGMATICS AND MASTER OF CANINICAL LAW*

TRUMPETERS
South American birds ARE TRAINED IN BRAZIL *TO STAND GUARD OVER OTHER POULTRY*

MOUNT CARMEL GUILD
A HOSPITAL FOR ALCOHOLICS in Paterson, N.J., IS LOCATED AT THE INTERSECTION OF *STRAIGHT AND NARROW STREETS*

The TRAIN That Goes To Sea

A RAILROAD TRACK LINKING THE GERMAN MAINLAND TO THE ISLAND OF SYLT, IN THE NORTH SEA, IS TRAVERSED FOR 7 MILES BY A TRAIN *THAT IS SPLASHED BY HIGH SEAS THROUGHOUT THE JOURNEY*

HO HUM

THE PARROT IS THE ONLY BIRD THAT YAWNS

CAPELUCHE OFFICIAL EXECUTIONER of Paris, France, SENTENCED TO DEATH HIMSELF IN 1418 AS A HIGHWAYMAN, NOTICED THAT HIS SUCCESSOR WAS NERVOUS —SO HE GAVE THE EXECUTIONER *INSTRUCTIONS BEFORE PUTTING HIS HEAD ON THE BLOCK*

REV. WILLIAM HENRY MILBURN
(1823-1903) AN ITINERANT PREACHER
TRAVELED 1,000,000 MILES
(200,000 MILES ON HORSEBACK)
-YET HE WAS TOTALLY BLIND

THE **CLOCK TOWER** OF THE
UNIVERSITY OF DETROIT
A BEAUTIFUL WAR MEMORIAL
ACTUALLY IS A DISGUISED SMOKESTACK

THE **SINGING SEAL**
MARJORY KENNEDY-FRASER
(1857-1930) FOLK SINGER OF HEBRIDEAN SONGS
SANG "THE SONG OF THE SEALS" TO A GROUP OF SEALS ON THE COAST OF THE HEBRIDES in the North Sea
AND ONE OF THE SEALS RESPONDED WITH SEVERAL NOTES OF THE SONG
-IN A PERFECT CONTRALTO

LARGEST TEA BUSH IN THE WORLD
A TEA BUSH at Taloen, Java, HAS A DIAMETER OF 36 FEET

ST. JOHN'S HOSPITAL in Angers, France, WAS CONSTRUCTED IN 1175 BY KING HENRY II OF ENGLAND TO ATONE FOR THE MURDER OF ARCHBISHOP THOMAS A BECKET

FEARSOME MONSTERS LEAD CHINESE FUNERALS *TO FRIGHTEN OFF ANY DEMONS THAT MIGHT ATTEMPT TO SEIZE THE DECEASED'S SOUL*

WHERE EVERY FARMER WORKS "THE ROCK PILE" SOME SOIL in Calabria, Italy, IS SO STONY THAT A PLOW MUST BE PULLED BY 12 OXEN *WHICH ARE LED BY A MULE*

THE STONE MAN NATURAL ROCK FORMATION

THE APPLE THAT MADE IBRAHIM COMMANDER OF EGYPT'S ARMY!

MOHAMMED ALI, ruler of Egypt, ANNOUNCED IN 1816 THAT HE WOULD GIVE COMMAND OF HIS ARMY TO WHOEVER COULD SECURE AN APPLE CENTERED ON A CARPET
- *WITHOUT SETTING FOOT ON THE CARPET*
AFTER EVERY OTHER CONTESTANT HAD FAILED, IBRAHIM REACHED THE APPLE *SIMPLY BY ROLLING UP THE CARPET*

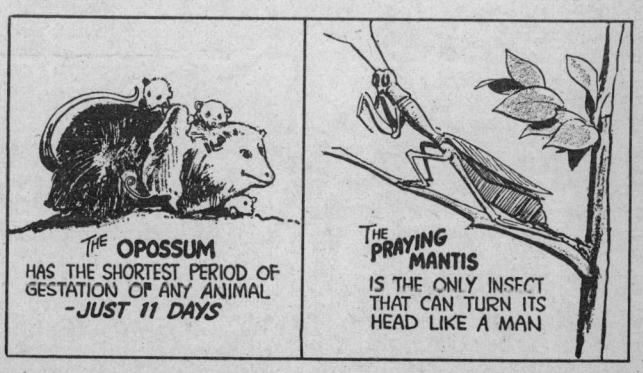

THE OPOSSUM HAS THE SHORTEST PERIOD OF GESTATION OF ANY ANIMAL - *JUST 11 DAYS*

THE PRAYING MANTIS IS THE ONLY INSECT THAT CAN TURN ITS HEAD LIKE A MAN

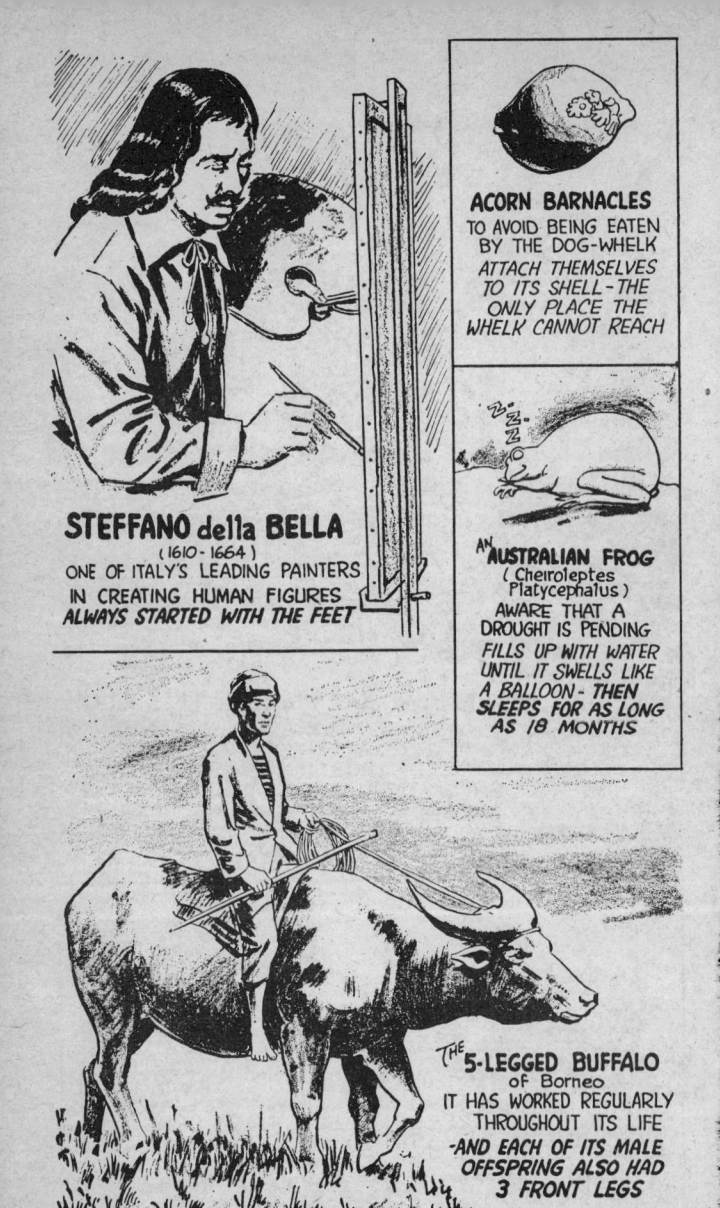

STEFFANO della BELLA
(1610-1664)
ONE OF ITALY'S LEADING PAINTERS IN CREATING HUMAN FIGURES *ALWAYS STARTED WITH THE FEET*

ACORN BARNACLES TO AVOID BEING EATEN BY THE DOG-WHELK *ATTACH THEMSELVES TO ITS SHELL – THE ONLY PLACE THE WHELK CANNOT REACH*

An **AUSTRALIAN FROG** (Cheiroleptes Platycephalus) AWARE THAT A DROUGHT IS PENDING *FILLS UP WITH WATER UNTIL IT SWELLS LIKE A BALLOON – THEN SLEEPS FOR AS LONG AS 18 MONTHS*

The **5-LEGGED BUFFALO** of Borneo IT HAS WORKED REGULARLY THROUGHOUT ITS LIFE –AND EACH OF ITS MALE OFFSPRING ALSO HAD **3 FRONT LEGS**

THE HOMES of the Chinantec Indians of Mexico, BECAUSE OF THE RAVAGES OF TERMITES, MUST BE *REBUILT EVERY YEAR*

ABRAHAM LINCOLN WAS THE FIRST U.S. PRESIDENT *BORN OUTSIDE THE ORIGINAL 13 STATES*

THE INGLIS MONUMENT at Chhatak, Assam, AN OBELISK HONORING THE BRITISH HERO OF AN INDIAN MUTINY WAS TURNED COMPLETELY AROUND BY A VIOLENT EARTHQUAKE A SECOND SHOCK LOOSENED THE TOP OF THE MONUMENT *-WHICH HAS BALANCED PRECARIOUSLY FOR 70 YEARS* -1897-

A **SOCKET** WAS DRILLED INTO A STONE IN ANCIENT BABYLONIA TO ENABLE DOORS TO SWING OPEN AND SHUT

THE CITY HALL
of Leonberg, Germany,
WAS CONSTRUCTED OF WOOD
YET IT ESCAPED UNHARMED IN
1895 WHEN FLAMES DESTROYED
3 HOUSES ON EITHER SIDE OF
IT AND ALL THE BUILDINGS
BEHIND IT

HOROZ ALI
THE LAST TURKISH GATEKEEPER
of Nicosia, Cyprus,
LIVED TO THE AGE OF 120

THOMIN (1519-1574)
JESTER IN THE COURTS
OF 3 FRENCH MONARCHS
WAS GIVEN THIS EPITAPH BY
FAMED POET PIERRE de RONSARD:
"HERE LIES THE WISEST
MAN IN ALL FRANCE"

A HYBRID FISH
Caught in England in 1928
WAS A CROSS BETWEEN A ROACH AND A RUDD

THE **NAVAL BATTLE** THAT WAS WON BY A PISTOL!

HIRAM PAULDING, A MIDSHIPMAN 17 YEARS OF AGE, ENABLED THE U.S. WAR SLOOP "TICONDEROGA" TO DEFEAT THE BRITISH SHIP "FINCH" *BY FIRING HIS PISTOL* LEARNING THAT THE "TICONDEROGA'S" GUNS COULD NOT BE FIRED FOR A LACK OF MATCHES, PAULDING SHOT HIS PISTOL INTO EACH GUN'S TOUCH HOLE — AND THE FLASHES SET OFF THE POWDER IN THE BIG GUNS (Sept. 11, 1814)

DILL SEEDS ARE NOT SEEDS AT ALL — THEY ARE THE RIPE FRUIT OF ANETHUM GRAVEOLENS

A **MIRAGE** SEEN IN THE ARCTIC SKY IN 1820 BY THE SCORESBY ARCTIC EXPEDITION **APPEARED AS A MULTI-TURRETED CASTLE**

85

WILLIAM LILLY (1602-1681) celebrated English astrologer SERVED AS AN OFFICIAL FORTUNE-TELLER IN THE ENGLISH ARMY -*TO IMPROVE MORALE BY PREDICTIONS OF VICTORY*

THE SACK TREE

THE UPAS TREE of India HAS AN INNER BARK WHICH IS USED TO MAKE *SACKS FOR THE TRANSPORTATION OF RICE*

THE CHURCH OF OUR LADY OF LARMOR near the harbor of L'Orient, France, HAS BEEN GIVEN **3** SALUTES BY THE GUNS OF EVERY FRENCH WARSHIP LEAVING THE PORT *FOR 300 YEARS*

FRENCH GALLEY SLAVES
in the 17th and 18th centuries
WERE PREVENTED FROM CRYING OUT DURING NAVAL BATTLES BY CORK PLUGS WHICH THEY WORE ON A STRING AROUND THEIR NECKS —AND WERE REQUIRED TO FORCE INTO THEIR OWN MOUTHS

THE **TOWER** of St. Germain Church in Tirlemont, Belgium, DAMAGED IN A WARTIME EXPLOSION, HAS BEEN LEFT IN A TILTED POSITION *FOR 174 YEARS*

THE **RIGHT HONORABLE PRIME MINISTER** *THE DUKE OF NEWCASTLE* (1693-1768) WHILE PRIME MINISTER OF GR. BRITAIN, DESPITE ALL THE COURT CONSPIRACIES OF THE PERIOD, *REFUSED TO READ ANY LETTER THAT WAS NOT ADDRESSED TO HIM*

THE **ROPE TREES** of Bega, in the Fiji Islands, GROW TWISTED TRUNKS THAT OFTEN MEASURE *500 FEET IN LENGTH*

SAFFRON AN AROMATIC COMPOUND USED BOTH AS COLORING MATTER AND AS A FLAVORER *REQUIRES A SEGMENT OF THE MINUTE STIGMAS OF 75,000 FLOWERS TO MAKE A SINGLE POUND*

CHRISTOPHER COLUMBUS HAD SNOW WHITE HAIR *AT THE AGE OF 30*

THE **SHEPHERD DOGS OF BERGAMO** in Italy ALWAYS HAVE ONE BLUE EYE AND ONE BROWN EYE

THE "RUBE GOLDBERG" STREET CAR

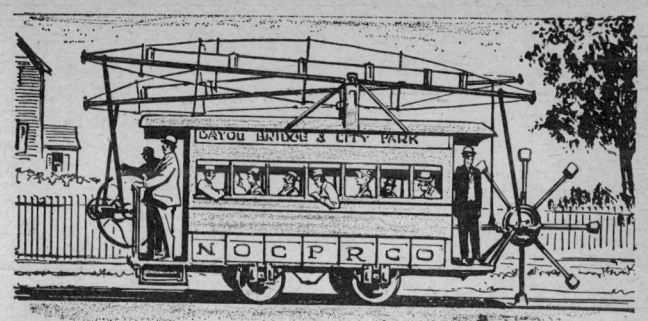

A TROLLEY used in New Orleans, La., in 1871 WAS OPERATED BY HAND BY A MOTORMAN WHO TURNED A WHEEL, WHICH SET IN MOTION SEVERAL OTHER WHEELS AND A "WALKING BEAM" ON THE ROOF, WHICH IN TURN REVOLVED A RIMLESS WHEEL WITH SPOKES - WHICH PUSHED THE CAR FORWARD
THE CAR WAS ABANDONED BECAUSE IT WORE OUT THE PAVEMENT

A 4-TINED FORK
USED IN THE FIJI ISLANDS WHEN THE NATIVES WERE **CANNIBALS**

THE QUEEN MOTHER
of Senya Beraku, on the Gulf of Guinea, West Africa, *IS NEITHER THE QUEEN NOR THE MOTHER OF THE KING - SHE IS THE KING'S SISTER - BUT HER SON SUCCEEDS TO THE THRONE WHEN THE MONARCH DIES*

NATIVE SOLDIERS IN THE FORMER GERMAN COLONY OF Tanganyika

WORE RAINCOATS THAT DOUBLED AS *TENTS*

MARKTOWN a community in Indiana WITH NARROW STREETS PATTERNED AFTER TOWNS IN SWITZERLAND *PARKS ITS CARS ON THE SIDEWALKS-AND THE PEOPLE WALK IN THE ROADWAY*

WITCH CHASERS

GLASS BALLS manufactured in the U.S. in the 19th century WERE HUNG IN THE WINDOWS OF HOMES TO WARD OFF THE EVIL DESIGNS OF WITCHES

PRINCE JOSEPH WENZEL (1718-1772) RULED LIECHTENSTEIN FOR 25 YEARS *-YET HE NEVER ONCE SET FOOT IN THAT PRINCIPALITY*

THE CHURCH of the ROCKS of MONT STE. ODILE in France
WAS ORIGINALLY BUILT AS THE VILLAGE CHURCH IN *THE ALSATIAN EXHIBIT AT THE PARIS WORLD'S FAIR OF 1925*

STONE SHAPED LIKE A WATERMELON

THE MAN WHO NEVER SLEPT IN BED
JOHN MIDDLETON (1789-1892) a peddler of Hartley, England, LIVED TO THE AGE OF 103 — AND SLEPT EVERY NIGHT OF HIS LIFE *IN A SHALLOW HOLE IN THE GROUND*

THE COFFIN of ST. CLEMENT INTO WHICH HIS BODY WAS PLACED IN 1140 *HAD PREVIOUSLY SERVED AS AN ANCIENT ETRUSCAN URN FOR 1,400 YEARS*

INDONESIAN WOMEN USE AS AN ORNAMENT TO DECORATE THEIR FOREHEADS, THE ARACHIS — *AN ORCHID SHAPED LIKE A BUG*

91

THE COMMUNAL TOWER in Ravenna, Italy, 130 FEET HIGH, HAS STOOD FOR 800 YEARS — *YET IT LEANS 3 FEET OFF LINE*

THE SEAMAN WHO WAS SAVED BY AN ALBATROSS

JOHN OAKLEY, HAVING FALLEN OVERBOARD FROM THE LINER "SOUTHERN CROSS" WAS NOT MISSED UNTIL THE BIG SHIP *WAS 20 MILES AWAY*

OAKLEY WOULD NEVER HAVE BEEN FOUND EXCEPT FOR A GIANT ALBATROSS WHICH THE SHIP'S CREW OBSERVED MAKING REPEATED SWOOPS AT THE BOBBING SAILOR - 1956

STRANGER CALL THIS NOT
A PLACE OF FEAR AND GLOOM
TO ME IT IS A PLEASANT SPOT
IT IS MY HUSBAND'S TOMB

Epitaph in Old Mandan Cemetery Near Bismarck, N.D.

PROFILE ROCK in Assonet, Mass., IS SAID TO BE A LIKENESS OF THE INDIAN MASSASOIT *WHO BEFRIENDED THE PILGRIMS IN 1621*

The **RESTLESS FLYCATCHER** of Australia IS ALSO CALLED "THE SCISSORS GRINDER" BECAUSE ITS CALL SOUNDS LIKE SHEARS AGAINST A GRINDING WHEEL

NEZAHUALCOYOTL the GREAT
KING OF ANAHUAC
(1403-1470) Mexico
WAS THE FATHER OF 60 SONS AND 50 DAUGHTERS

COUNT von FÜRSTENBERG
(1629-1704)
DIED IN PARIS, FRANCE, OF STARVATION BECAUSE HE WAS TOO STINGY TO BUY FOOD — YET HE HAD AN ANNUAL INCOME OF $136,000

408² EQUALS **166464** - REVERSING THE ORIGINAL NUMBER - 804² RESULTS IN A REVERSAL OF THE THREE PAIRS OF DIGITS - **646416**

A **HUGE SHIPYARD** near Pornic, France, WAS SOLD IN 1819 FOR A SUM COMPRISING $1.95 A YEAR— *THE YARD WAS CLOSED AFTER 10 YEARS AND PAYMENTS TOTALLING $19.50*

THE **ANTENNA MEN OF THE ZAMBESI VALLEY**

ILA TRIBESMEN of Africa WIND THEIR HAIR AROUND THE HORN OF A SABLE ANTELOPE UNTIL THEY HAVE A BOBBING ANTENNA **3 FEET LONG**

THE **GRAVE** OF A WIFE in Misunda, Gabon, Africa, DECORATED WITH THE USUAL HOUSEHOLD UTENSILS AND ALSO HER HUSBAND'S HUNTING RIFLE -TO INDICATE HE NO LONGER HAS A REASON TO PROVIDE FOOD

THE SEEDCASE OF A PLANT CALLED THE GOAT'S BEARD *RESEMBLES A PARACHUTE*

WANG HOU CHUNG WAS KEEPER OF DOGS AND HAWKS FOR CHINESE EMPEROR TAO KU'S FAMILY *FOR 75 YEARS*

GRAPHITE WHICH PROVIDES THE LEAD IN PENCILS WAS CONSIDERED SO VALUABLE IN ANCIENT ENGLAND THAT STEALING IT WAS PUNISHABLE BY *A YEAR IN PRISON AND A PUBLIC WHIPPING*

THE "**BARCLAY**" A WHALESHIP OUT OF New Bedford, Mass., WHICH MADE 20 VOYAGES OVER A PERIOD OF 64 YEARS, WAS AWAY FROM ITS HOME PORT ON ONE TRIP *FOR 65 MONTHS*

THE GREAT HOUSE THAT WAS DESTROYED BY GREED

THE PALACE OF ARKHANGELSKOYE, in Russia WAS RAZED BY FIRE BECAUSE ITS OWNER, PRINCE NICHOLAS YUSUPOV, TO AVOID WASTING WOOD, HEATED THE ESTATE BY BURNING SAWDUST *WHICH EXPLODED—*

HE WAS ONE OF THE RICHEST MEN OF HIS TIME AND OWNED HUNDREDS OF THOUSANDS OF ACRES OF FOREST

THE REV. JOHN BUZZELL (1768-1863) of Portland, Me., WAS A PREACHER *FOR 76 YEARS*

A **WHITE CROW** considered sacred by the Burmese Government WAS GIVEN ITS OWN PALACE, AN ATTENDANT WITH THE CABINET RANK OF MINISTER OF STATE, AND UPON ITS DEATH IN 1927 *WAS ACCORDED A ROYAL FUNERAL*

THE TRIGGERFISH JAMS ITSELF INTO A HOLE —AND THEN ERECTS A SPIKE ON ITS BACK SO IT CANNOT BE PULLED OUT

A FISHERMAN MUST DEPRESS A "CATCH" BEHIND THE SPIKE TO RELEASE IT

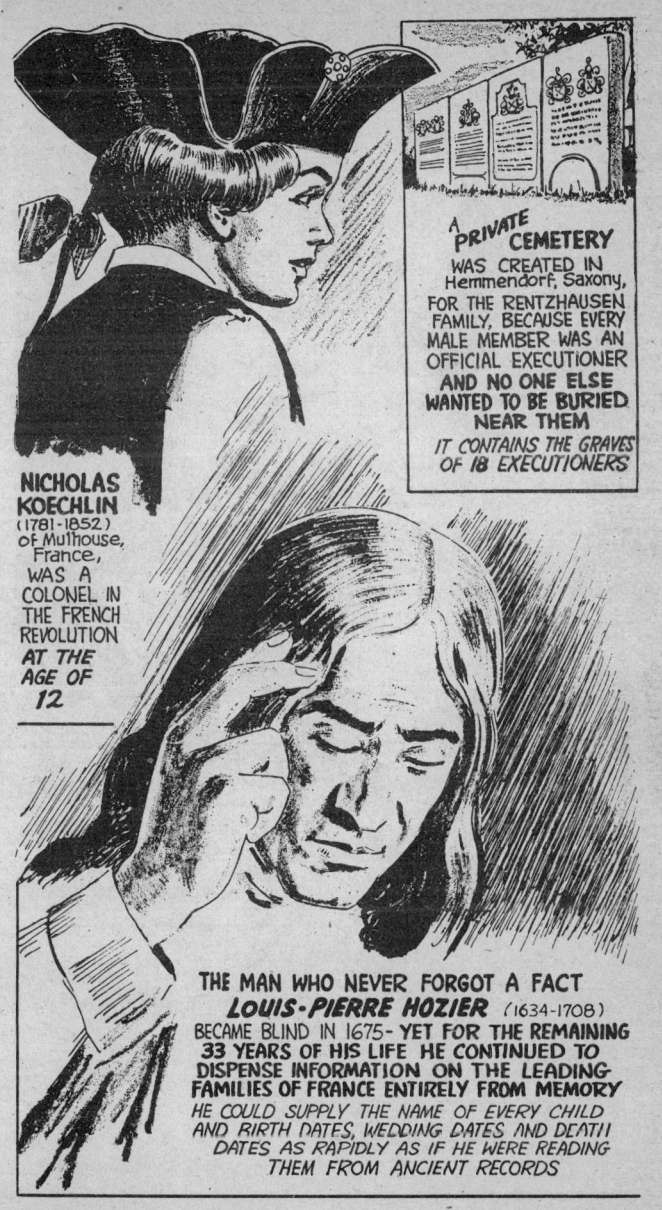

A **PRIVATE CEMETERY** WAS CREATED IN Hemmendorf, Saxony, FOR THE RENTZHAUSEN FAMILY, BECAUSE EVERY MALE MEMBER WAS AN OFFICIAL EXECUTIONER AND NO ONE ELSE WANTED TO BE BURIED NEAR THEM
IT CONTAINS THE GRAVES OF 18 EXECUTIONERS

NICHOLAS KOECHLIN (1781-1852) of Mulhouse, France, WAS A COLONEL IN THE FRENCH REVOLUTION *AT THE AGE OF 12*

THE MAN WHO NEVER FORGOT A FACT
LOUIS-PIERRE HOZIER (1634-1708) BECAME BLIND IN 1675 - YET FOR THE REMAINING 33 YEARS OF HIS LIFE HE CONTINUED TO DISPENSE INFORMATION ON THE LEADING FAMILIES OF FRANCE ENTIRELY FROM MEMORY
HE COULD SUPPLY THE NAME OF EVERY CHILD AND BIRTH DATES, WEDDING DATES AND DEATH DATES AS RAPIDLY AS IF HE WERE READING THEM FROM ANCIENT RECORDS

THE HANDLE TREE

A PEAR TREE near Neubudzen, Prussia, WAS REGULARLY CLIMBED BY THE ILL IN THE BELIEF THAT SLIDING THROUGH THE OPENING WAS *A CURE FOR ANY AILMENT*

ADMIRAL CHARLES FLEEMING (1774-1840)

WHO JOINED THE BRITISH NAVY AT THE AGE OF 11 AND FILLED EVERY RANK FROM MIDSHIPMAN TO ADMIRAL *NEVER ACCEPTED PAYMENT FOR HIS SERVICES*

YOUNG GIRLS in Nazare, Portugal, ARE NEVER WELL DRESSED WITHOUT *AT LEAST 7 PETTICOATS*

The ASPARAGUS BEETLE
CARRIES ON ITS BACK *THE OUTLINE OF A LIZARD*

The CLOISTER
OF ST. ANTHONY OF GALAMUS the East Pyrenees, France, IS IN THE SHADOW OF A 50-FOOT-HIGH FIGURE OF THAT SAINT *ETCHED INTO THE SOLID ROCK BY NATURE*

The ASTROLOGER WHO WAS **DEAD WRONG!**

MICHEL NOSTRADAMUS, Jr. TRIED TO FOLLOW IN THE FOOTSTEPS OF HIS FAMOUS FATHER, *BUT HIS PROPHECIES WERE NEVER RIGHT* — HE PREDICTED POUZIN, FRANCE, WOULD BE BURNED IN A SIEGE AND WHEN IT WAS SPARED HE SET IT AFIRE HIMSELF. ENRAGED, THE TOWN'S COMMANDER ASKED YOUNG NOSTRADAMUS IF HE EXPECTED TO LIVE ANOTHER DAY — AND WHEN THE ASTROLOGER SAID HE WOULD, *THE COMMANDER KILLED HIM* (1574)

The BLACK WINGED STILT
IN PROPORTION TO ITS SIZE *HAS THE LONGEST LEGS OF ANY BIRD*

ULU ATU TEMPLE in Bali
LOCATED ATOP A CLIFF 300 FEET HIGH IS THE SITE OF REGULAR SERVICES ALTHOUGH THE GROUND IS SLOWLY ERODING AWAY AND *IT SOON WILL PLUNGE INTO THE SEA*

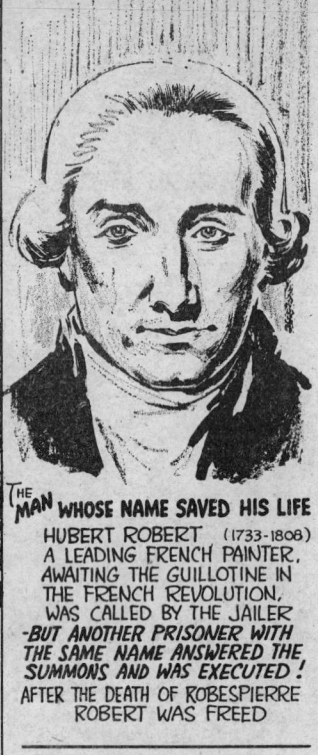

THE MAN WHOSE NAME SAVED HIS LIFE
HUBERT ROBERT (1733-1808) A LEADING FRENCH PAINTER, AWAITING THE GUILLOTINE IN THE FRENCH REVOLUTION, WAS CALLED BY THE JAILER —BUT ANOTHER PRISONER WITH THE SAME NAME ANSWERED THE SUMMONS AND WAS EXECUTED! AFTER THE DEATH OF ROBESPIERRE ROBERT WAS FREED

THE CANAL-PORTAGE RAILROAD WHICH LINKED Philadelphia, Pa., and Pittsburgh in 1840
TRANSPORTED BOATS BY RAILROAD FROM PHILADELPHIA TO COLUMBIA, SAILED THEM VIA CANAL TO HOLLIDAYSBURG, SLID THEM DOWN 11 SKIDS TO JOHNSTOWN AND THEN FLOATED THEM TO PITTSBURGH

THE MAN WHO LOST A GOLD MINE

ISAAC ALDEN of Willow Creek, Colo., FOUND A PIECE OF ORE HE THOUGHT WAS COPPER IN 1880 -- BUT IT WAS ASSAYED AS GOLD WORTH $1,600 A TON! A FOREST FIRE HAD DESTROYED ALL LANDMARKS IN THE AREA AND ALDEN NEVER WAS ABLE TO RELOCATE HIS GOLD MINE, ALTHOUGH HE SEARCHED FOR 40 YEARS

JEAN FRANÇOIS PEYRUSSE (1747-1822) AS A REWARD FOR CREATING A NEW RECIPE FOR KING LOUIS XVIII OF FRANCE, WAS MADE A DUKE AND MASTER OF THE ROYAL HOUSEHOLD -- YET THE FIRST TIME PEYRUSSE TRIED THE CONCOCTION HIMSELF HE DIED OF INDIGESTION

THE **TAMBOURINE DOVE** of Africa MAKES A SOUND LIKE A *TOM-TOM*

ANTOINE MONEUSE
a farmer of St. Vaast, Belgium,
WAS SHOT TO DEATH BY A
NEIGHBOR IN A QUARREL IN 1779,
BUT HIS WIFE, CATHERINE, REFUSED
TO IDENTIFY HIS REMAINS
*SO SHE WOULD NOT HAVE
TO WEAR WIDOW'S WEEDS*

A **SINGLE PIECE OF FURNITURE**
Patented in the U.S. in 1866
IS A COMBINATION BED,
BUREAU –AND PIANO

Sunflower
GROWING
OUT OF
ANOTHER
SUNFLOWER
BLOSSOM

"MISSIOD ANNOUNCES TO HIS HIGHNESS THAT HE IS DEAD"

A **TARTAR** SERVANT OF PRINCE
YUSUPOV, of St. Petersburg,
AWARE THAT HE WAS ON HIS
DEATHBED IN THE CRIMEA, WIRED
*THE ABOVE PREMATURE NOTICE
OF HIS OWN DEATH* (1908)

A BRIDGE
CONSTRUCTED OVER THE WHANGPO RIVER, CHINA, IN 1880, HAS BEEN USED BY TRAVELERS WITHOUT IMPROVEMENT FOR 87 YEARS - YET IT CONSISTS ONLY OF **SINGLE BAMBOO POLES LAID END TO END**

THE RESCUE PARTY THAT WAS GUIDED BY A DREAM!

THE REV. LEONARD H. WHEELER of La Pointe, Wis., MAROONED WITH 2 INDIANS ON A REMOTE ISLAND ON LAKE SUPERIOR WHEN THEIR CANOE WAS WRECKED, WAS SAVED WHEN THE MINISTER'S WIFE, RHODA, SAW HER HUSBAND AND HIS GUIDES WITH A SMASHED CANOE ON THE ISLAND - *IN A DREAM!*

THE PRAYING MANTIS CAN FLY, CLEAN ITSELF AND BUILD A NEST *AFTER ITS HEAD HAS BEEN CUT OFF*

THE CLIFFORD INN London, England, *IS NOT AN INN* IT IS A LAW SCHOOL, AND THE STRUCTURE WAS ORIGINALLY GRANTED TO THE CLIFFORD FAMILY BY KING EDWARD II, IN 1310, *FOR AN ANNUAL RENTAL OF ONE PENNY*

TODA TRIBESMEN of Southern India GREET THE SUN REVERENTLY EACH MORNING *BY PLACING THEIR THUMBS UNDER THEIR NOSES AND SPREADING THEIR FINGERS*

THE GLASS HOUSE A TURRETED "CASTLE" in Wetaskiwin, Alberta, *BUILT ENTIRELY WITH BOTTLES* THE STRUCTURE IS 42 FEET BY 38 FEET AND CONSTRUCTED OF **93,000** LONG-NECKED BOTTLES

THE PALE CLOUDED YELLOW BUTTERFLY IS FOUND ON THE SHORES OF THE SOUTHERN MEDITERRANEAN — BUT ONCE EVERY DECADE *SWARMS OF THEM FLY TO ENGLAND* IT IS BELIEVED THEY ARE OBEYING AN ANCIENT INSTINCT DATING FROM THE TIME ENGLAND WAS A SUB-TROPICAL COUNTRY

THE CYCLOPS
A TINY FRESH-WATER CRUSTACEAN *CARRIES ITS EGGS IN 2 POUCHES*

FRIEDRICH NAUSEA
(1480-1550)
THE RENOWNED GERMAN DIPLOMAT ADOPTED THAT SURNAME AFTER HAVING CHANGED HIS ORIGINAL NAME, ECKEL— THE GERMAN WORD FOR DISGUST —TO UNRATH **WHICH MEANS GARBAGE—** HE THEN CHANGED HIS NAME TO NAUSEA

DEAREST TOM
THOU ART GONE
THY KIND HEART
I MISS
YOU DID NOT SAY
GOODBYE TOM
NOR GIVE ME THE
PARTING KISS

Tombstone in Laurel Hill Cemetery, San Francisco, Calif.

SCHOOLCHILDREN
of Ravensburg, Germany, ANNUALLY MARCH SWINGING LONG SWITCHES —TO COMMEMORATE THE 14TH CENTURY PLAGUE WHEN EVERYONE WAS SO AFRAID OF CATCHING THE DISEASE THEY WAVED LONG TWIGS AT EACH OTHER INSTEAD OF SHAKING HANDS

BOYS' DAY
IS CELEBRATED ANNUALLY IN JAPAN BY FLYING FOR EACH BOY IN THE HOUSEHOLD A REPLICA OF A CARP – THE CARP'S DETERMINATION IN SWIMMING UPSTREAM HAS MADE IT THE SYMBOL OF RUGGED MANHOOD

COUNT CHAROLAIS
(1700-1760) A COUSIN OF KING LOUIS XV OF FRANCE WAS SO CRUEL THAT HIS GREATEST PLEASURE WAS PUSHING *ROOFERS TO THEIR DEATH!* THE KING REFORMED HIM BY ISSUING A DECREE PLEDGING *A PARDON TO WHOEVER MIGHT MURDER THE COUNT*

LOBI TRIBESMEN
of the Upper Volta, Africa, USE THEIR BOWS BOTH AS WEAPONS *AND AS MUSICAL INSTRUMENTS*

A HOT TIP
"COOL," A HORSE RACING AT Haydock Park, Liverpool, England, WAS BET ON OUT OF PITY BY A WOMAN IN NOVEMBER, 1929, BECAUSE NO ONE ELSE HAD WAGERED ON THE ENTRY- *COOL WON AND PAID HER 3,410 TO 1*

THE "EXTERNESTEINE"
AN ARMED GERMAN TRAWLER THAT BECAME WEDGED IN THE ICE OFF GREENLAND *WAS THE ONLY GERMAN SURFACE WARSHIP CAPTURED INTACT BY AMERICAN FORCES IN WORLD WAR II*

VALERIA CUPOLA
A ROMAN ACTRESS OF THE 1ST CENTURY B.C.
APPEARED ON THE STAGE *FOR 91 YEARS*

THE FIRST PARLIAMENT BUILDING in Japan
WAS DESTROYED BY FIRE IN 1891 *ON THE DAY IT OPENED ITS DOORS FOR THE FIRST TIME*

HERMAN and ANNTJE POLEMUS WERE MARRIED IN Johannesburg, So. Africa, *INSIDE A LION CAGE* (1895)

PORDENONE (1484-1540) ONE OF THE FOREMOST PAINTERS OF HIS TIME WAS SO FEARFUL OF JEALOUS RIVALS THAT HE ALWAYS PAINTED WEARING A SWORD AND USING A BRUSH THAT HAD IN ITS HANDLE **A DAGGER** —HE DIED BY POISONING

A **WATCH** MADE IN SWITZERLAND IN 1800 *IN THE SHAPE OF A BUTTERFLY WITH JEWELED WINGS*

2 TYPES OF AUSTRALIAN ORCHIDS GROW AND ACTUALLY BLOOM *BENEATH THE SOIL*

THE VENUS FLY TRAP

SNAPS SHUT ITS LEAVES ON AN INSECT —THEN KILLS IT WITH A CHARGE OF ELECTRICITY

THE HEAVIEST MILITARY UNIFORMS IN HISTORY

THE SULTAN'S GUARD IN 17th-CENTURY TURKEY, WORE AS AN ADORNMENT A STUFFED TIGER WEIGHING 100 POUNDS— THE FULL ARMOR OF A KNIGHT WEIGHED ONLY ABOUT 70 POUNDS

MADONNA AND CHILD
STALAGMITE IN THE GIRLS' GROTTO in the Cevennes Mountains, France

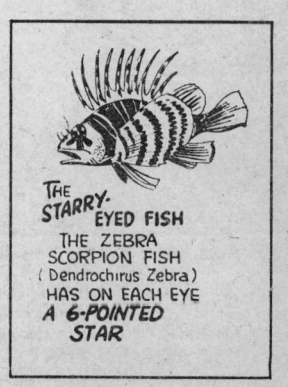

THE STARRY-EYED FISH
THE ZEBRA SCORPION FISH (Dendrochirus Zebra) HAS ON EACH EYE A 6-POINTED STAR

PTE. PEPIN
of Paris, France,
A MERCHANT IMPLICATED IN AN ATTEMPT TO ASSASSINATE KING LOUIS PHILIPPE, WAS GRIPPING HIS CHURCHWARDEN PIPE SO TIGHTLY WHEN HE WAS GUILLOTINED THAT *HIS HEAD WAS BURIED WITH THE PIPE STILL CLENCHED IN HIS TEETH* (Feb. 19, 1836)

THREE LAND PEAK
10,500 FEET HIGH
IS LOCATED IN 3 STATES
SWITZERLAND, VORARLBERG AND TYROL

THE HEDDAUA BROTHERHOOD
A RELIGIOUS ORDER OF MENDICANTS in Beni Aros, Morocco,
HAVE NOT EATEN A MEAL FOR 197 YEARS UNTIL THEY HAVE FIRST THROWN PART OF THEIR FOOD INTO THE MEHASEN RIVER
- *TO FEED THE FISH*

110

THE ARCH OF TAMUDA
in an abandoned town in Morocco
HAD ALL OF ITS MORTAR WASHED AWAY CENTURIES AGO - YET *IS STILL STANDING*

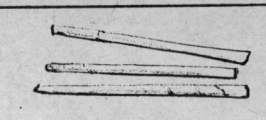

THE FIRST MATCH
A MATCH INVENTED IN 1805 WAS MADE OF A WOOD SPLINTER WITH A HEAD CONSISTING OF POTASH, SUGAR AND GUM - WHICH WAS IGNITED AGAINST ASBESTOS SOAKED IN SULPHURIC ACID

A BIRD'S NEST
of 4 stories
BUILT BY A YELLOW WARBLER IN ITS ATTEMPTS TO THWART THE INTRUSIONS OF A COWBIRD THAT WANTED *THE WARBLER TO HATCH THE COWBIRD'S EGGS*

WOMEN of Guinea
GATHER ANNUALLY IN THE SACRED FOREST OF MACETA FOR A TRIBAL DANCE THAT LASTS FROM SUNRISE TO MIDNIGHT - *EACH MOTHER CARRYING A CHILD STRAPPED TO HER BACK*

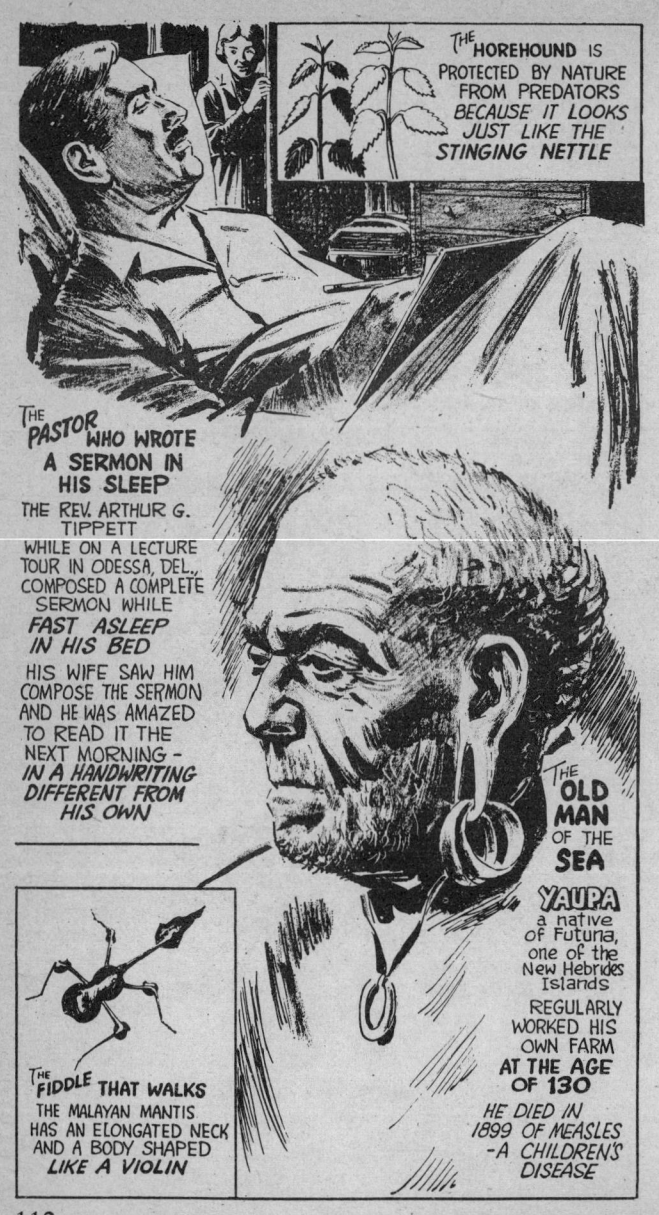

The HOREHOUND IS PROTECTED BY NATURE FROM PREDATORS *BECAUSE IT LOOKS JUST LIKE THE STINGING NETTLE*

The PASTOR WHO WROTE A SERMON IN HIS SLEEP

THE REV. ARTHUR G. TIPPETT WHILE ON A LECTURE TOUR IN ODESSA, DEL., COMPOSED A COMPLETE SERMON WHILE *FAST ASLEEP IN HIS BED*

HIS WIFE SAW HIM COMPOSE THE SERMON AND HE WAS AMAZED TO READ IT THE NEXT MORNING – *IN A HANDWRITING DIFFERENT FROM HIS OWN*

The FIDDLE THAT WALKS
THE MALAYAN MANTIS HAS AN ELONGATED NECK AND A BODY SHAPED *LIKE A VIOLIN*

The OLD MAN OF THE SEA
YAUPA a native of Futuna, one of the New Hebrides Islands

REGULARLY WORKED HIS OWN FARM AT THE AGE OF 130

HE DIED IN 1899 OF MEASLES – *A CHILDREN'S DISEASE*

The PEBBLE PLANT of South Africa PRODUCES FRUIT THAT LOOKS SO MUCH LIKE PEBBLES, EVEN HUNGRY ANIMALS AND BIRDS PASS IT BY

The EGGS of Hydrocrurius Punctatus A GIANT WATERBUG OF Madagascar ARE CARRIED UNTIL THEY HATCH *ON THE BACK OF THE FATHER*

THE BELFRY TOP of the Church of Our Lady of Roz Madou, in Camaret, France, BLOWN OFF BY AN INVADING ARMY IN 1694, *HAS NOT BEEN REPAIRED, AS A MEMORIAL TO THAT BATTLE, FOR 273 YEARS*

LIVIUS GEMINIUS a member of the Roman Senate WAS REWARDED WITH 1,000,000 SESTERCES ($40,000) BY EMPEROR CALIGULA BECAUSE LIVIUS REPORTED *A DREAM IN WHICH THE EMPEROR'S SISTER ASCENDED TO HEAVEN*

BABY SEA ELEPHANTS on the Prince Edward Islands, South Africa, CAN ONLY DIGEST THEIR FOOD WHEN THEY ARE *SUBMERGED IN WATER*

THE SHIP THAT WAS SAVED BY A PIECE OF STONE

THE "SAN STEFANO" a Maltese galleon, WAS DRIVEN ONTO THE ROCKS OFF LIVORNO, ITALY, WITH SUCH FORCE *THAT A HOLE WAS TORN IN ITS HULL*— THE VESSEL WAS BLOWN FREE BY A SHIFTING WIND AND REMAINED BUOYANT **BECAUSE A PIECE OF ROCK WAS TIGHTLY WEDGED IN THE HOLE** (1552)

RAYMOND PHELYPEAUX
(1560-1629) French Secretary of State
BEQUEATHED HIS OFFICE IN 1621 TO HIS MALE DESCENDANTS *WHO OCCUPIED IT FOR AN UNINTERRUPTED PERIOD OF 156 YEARS*

THE **CASTLE of VERDALA** on the island of Malta WAS BUILT ENTIRELY FROM THE STONE *EXCAVATED FOR ITS FOUNDATION*

THE CEMETERY THAT HAS NO GRAVES

THE GRASIAS of India CREMATE THEIR DEAD AND SCATTER THE ASHES -BUT A YEAR LATER ERECT A TOMBSTONE AS A MEMORIAL TO THE DEPARTED

BENVENUTO CELLINI (1500-1571) CARVED HIS OWN PORTRAIT ON THE BACK OF AN ANCIENT STATUE OF PERSEUS *BECAUSE HE DREAMED THAT HE WAS AN INCARNATION OF THE GREEK PHILOSOPHER*

YAKS DRIVEN IN CARAVANS in the Himalayas HAVE NO HARNESS OR REINS AND ARE STEERED TO THE RIGHT OR LEFT *BY THROWING ROCKS AT THEM*

THE LEANING TOWER of DAUSENAU
Germany
IS 4 FEET OUT OF LINE

1st SERGEANT CORBETT MEEKS
of Fort Sam Houston, Texas,
IN 29 YEARS OF SERVICE WAS
AWARDED **61** DECORATIONS

THE COLD BUG (Grylloblatta)
A WINGLESS INSECT OF
THE CANADIAN ROCKIES
THRIVES IN FRIGID
TEMPERATURES—AND PERISHES
WHEN THE MERCURY CLIMBS
TO 15 DEGREES ABOVE FREEZING

THE MOUNT MELLERAY ABBEY
a Trappist monastery in Ireland
MAINTAINS AN INN WHICH OFFERS ANY TRAVELER
LODGING AND FOOD FOR A WEEK WITHOUT CHARGE

THE **BELFRY** of the Church of Collioure, France, *ALSO SERVES AS A LIGHTHOUSE*

THE **FAVORITE** "TIME CLOCK" during the Middle Ages WAS A QUADRUPLE HOUR GLASS —COMPRISING AN HOUR GLASS, A ¾-HOUR GLASS, A ½-HOUR GLASS AND A QUARTER-HOUR GLASS

The **GAY WIDOW** DIANE DE POITIERS (1499-1566) WHO LOST HER HUSBAND IN 1531 BECAME A FAVORITE COMPANION OF KING HENRY II AND LED A GAY LIFE AT THE MONARCH'S COURT *BUT ALWAYS DRESSED IN MOURNING FOR 35 YEARS*

117

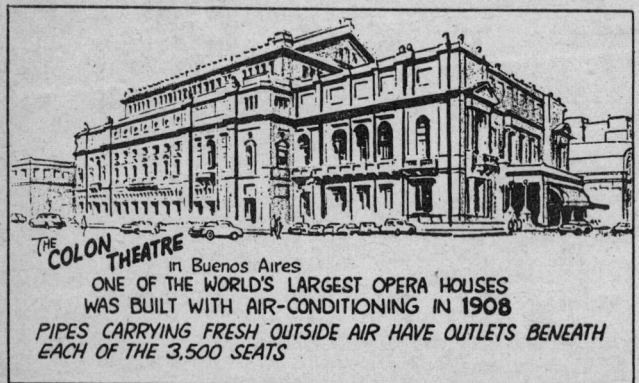

IDA MAY WHITESIDE and EDWARD WHITESIDE of Asheville, N.C.,
BOTH DIED ON THEIR BIRTHDAY
IDA MAY DIED IN 1908 - AND HER HUSBAND IN 1930

THE **FIRST MOUNTED POLICE** in British Borneo *RODE BUFFALOES*

THE **COLON THEATRE** in Buenos Aires
ONE OF THE WORLD'S LARGEST OPERA HOUSES WAS BUILT WITH AIR-CONDITIONING IN 1908
PIPES CARRYING FRESH OUTSIDE AIR HAVE OUTLETS BENEATH EACH OF THE 3,500 SEATS

THE PULPIT of the CHURCH OF IRRSEE, in Austria, IS A REPLICA OF THE SPANISH FLAGSHIP WHICH DEFEATED THE TURKS IN A SEA BATTLE OFF LEPANTO, GREECE, *396 YEARS AGO*

THE MAN WHO WAS KILLED BY HIS CONSCIENCE!
DEY KURD ABDI - Ruler of Algeria, WAS SO REMORSEFUL AFTER HE HAD REFUSED MILITARY AID TO AN ALLY, THAT HE FASTED FOR **64** DAYS - AND FINALLY DIED OF STARVATION

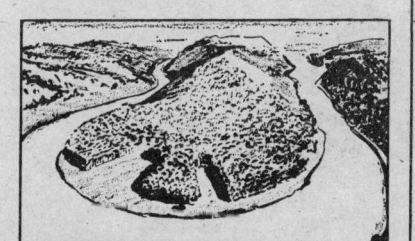

THE SAAR RIVER near Metlach, Germany, FLOWS IN ALMOST A PERFECT CIRCLE

A **SAILING SHIP MODEL** MADE BY FRENCH WAR PRISONERS in England *ENTIRELY FROM OLD BEEF BONES - WITH THE RIGGING MADE FROM THEIR OWN HAIR* (1798)

EGG
THE SIZE AND SHAPE OF A *PEANUT*

SCHOOLTEACHERS

in 18th-century Europe SHOWED THEIR TEACHING QUALIFICATIONS *BY THE NUMBER OF GOOSE FEATHERS IN THEIR HATS—* ONE FEATHER INDICATED A TEACHER OF READING, 2 MEANT AN INSTRUCTOR QUALIFIED IN READING AND WRITING, AND 3 FEATHERS IDENTIFIED A MASTER OF **READING, WRITING AND ARITHMETIC**

WOMEN of Gialo, in the Libyan Desert, WEAR CAPES WITH A TRAIN 2 YARDS LONG *TO WIPE OUT THEIR FOOTPRINTS AND THUS FOIL EFFORTS BY THE DEVIL TO TRAIL AND TEMPT THEM*

"MERRICK"
an American race horse that died in 1941 HAD THE LONGEST LIFE OF ANY REGISTERED HORSE - **38 YEARS**
IT WON 61 RACES AND FINISHED SECOND 40 TIMES IN 205 RACES

THE **SEA MAT** APPEARS TO BE SEAWEED, BUT ACTUALLY IT IS A COLONY OF ANIMALS - *EACH IN A HOME WITH ITS OWN DOOR* - WHEN PLACED IN THE SEA THE DOORS OPEN AND HUNDREDS OF MOUTHS PROTRUDE

BRIDGES
ARE BUILT BY THE NGONIS OF AFRICA BY FELLING TREES FROM BOTH BANKS **SO THAT THEIR BRANCHES INTERLOCK ACROSS A STREAM** *THE TREES ARE THEN LASHED TOGETHER WITH STRIPS OF BARK*

TIME'S A'WASTIN'

Richard **HACKETT** of Bayshore, N.Y. PLAYING BASKETBALL FOR THE OUR LADY OF GRACE JUNIORS DEFEATED THE ST. THOMAS APOSTLE TEAM TWICE IN ONE SEASON BY SCORING A BASKET IN THE FINAL **20 SECONDS OF PLAY** - *EACH TIME WINNING THE GAME BY A SCORE OF* **39 TO 37**

A CHAPEL
CONSTRUCTED FROM THE RUINS OF THE ROMAN TOWN OF SALA STANDS AS A MEMORIAL TO THE COMMUNITY WHICH *WAS DESTROYED BY THE HUNS 1,515 YEARS AGO*

GENERAL PHIL KEARNY
(1814-1862) WHOSE LEFT ARM WAS AMPUTATED IN THE MEXICAN WAR, SERVED IN THE NORTHERN CAVALRY IN THE CIVIL WAR
WIELDING A SABER IN HIS RIGHT HAND AND GRIPPING THE REINS IN HIS TEETH

RACHEL JACKSON wife of President Andrew Jackson, AT THE ADVICE OF HER DOCTOR RELIEVED HER BRONCHIAL CONDITION BY *SMOKING A CORNCOB PIPE*

A **NEW RAILROAD BRIDGE** ACROSS THE WOURI RIVER, in the Cameroons, Africa, BECAUSE OF THE ODD LOCATION OF SAND BARS *HAS A SHARP CURVE IN THE MIDDLE OF THE RIVER*

THE **DEAD** in the Pauwi Tribe of New Guinea ARE LEFT IN A CANOE RESTING ON A HIGH PLATFORM - SURROUNDED BY ALL HIS WORLDLY POSSESSIONS - IN THE BELIEF THAT THEIR SPIRITS WILL THUS BE PREPARED TO *WEATHER THE 2ND GREAT FLOOD*

A **BRIDE** in Bali DURING HER WEDDING CEREMONY MUST WEAVE, SPIN AND COOK *TO DEMONSTRATE TO HER MOTHER-IN-LAW THAT SHE IS READY FOR MARRIAGE*

THE **LITTLE BLACKBIRD OF THE ISLES** CAN BE FOUND ONLY ON THE TINY ISLAND OF COUSIN, IN THE INDIAN OCEAN

THE HIGHEST SHIP TOLL IN HISTORY

THE "KOMET" A NAZI RAIDER TO PASS THROUGH THE SOVIET-CONTROLLED NORTHERN SEA ROUTE TO THE PACIFIC IN JULY, 1940, PAID A TOLL OF **$400,000**

IT ENABLED THE "KOMET" TO SINK 10 ALLIED SHIPS, WITH A CARGO OF 64,000 TONS

THE BAPTISMAL FONT of the Church of Lodi, Italy, HAD BEEN CONVERTED INTO A PUBLIC FOUNTAIN AS A **MONUMENT TO THE THOUSANDS OF CHILDREN BAPTIZED IN IT OVER THE CENTURIES**

THE SHELL THAT WORKS ITS OWNER TO DEATH

THE AUGER SHELL of New Caledonia GROWS SO LONG AND HEAVY *THAT THE MOLLUSK WHICH MUST DRAG IT ALONG THE SAND DIES OF EXHAUSTION*

AGHA MIR

PRIME MINISTER TO KING GHAZI-UD-DIN, of Oudh, India, from 1814 to 1827 PAID HIMSELF AN ANNUAL SALARY OF 33 MILLION RUPEES - $10,560,000 - *DEPOSED BY A NEW MONARCH HE CARRIED AWAY FROM OUDH ENOUGH TREASURE* **TO FILL 800 BULLOCK CARTS**

A DEAD SHARK SINKS SO SLOWLY THAT ITS BODY IS ALMOST COMPLETELY DISSOLVED BY THE SALT WATER BEFORE IT REACHES THE BOTTOM OF THE SEA — THE ONLY PART OF THE SHARK THAT IS IMPERVIOUS TO THE ACTION OF THE SALT IS ITS TEETH

MOUNT MONTUZZA in Trieste, Italy, CAN BE ASCENDED BY *A ZIG-ZAG STAIRWAY*

THE **COLONEL** of the IMPERIAL CUIRASSIER REGIMENT WAS THE ONLY ARMY OFFICER PRIVILEGED FOR A PERIOD OF 299 YEARS TO CALL UPON THE AUSTRIAN EMPEROR *WEARING BOOTS AND SPURS AND UNANNOUNCED* — THIS WAS A REWARD HONORING THE REGIMENT THAT HAD SAVED THE EMPEROR'S LIFE IN 1619

A **COIN** MINTED IN CAUCASIAN GEORGIA (1184-1212) ESPECIALLY FOR THE PURCHASE OF BEVERAGES *WAS SHAPED LIKE A BOTTLE*

THE JEST THAT JILTED DEATH

THE DUKE de LAUZUN ON HIS DEATH BED IN 1721 DECIDED TO PLAY A FINAL JOKE ON HIS ASSEMBLED HEIRS BY ANNOUNCING HE WAS LEAVING HIS FORTUNE TO CHARITY— THE SURPRISED LOOK ON THEIR FACES MADE THE DUKE LAUGH SO HEARTILY THAT HE RECOVERED HIS HEALTH—AND LIVED TO THE AGE OF 90!

THE ADMINISTRATIVE OFFICE of the National Library in Paris, France, ORIGINALLY WAS A PALACE WHICH JULES MAZARIN, THE FRENCH STATESMAN, WON IN 1644 FROM ITS OWNER *IN A GAME OF CARDS*

GIANT STRAWBERRIES ARE STRUNG TOGETHER BY THE STEMS in Colombia, So. Amer., *AND SOLD BY THE YARD*

THE **MINING WASP** (Odynerus geminus) EXCAVATES A TUNNEL AND TOPS IT WITH A TURRET—THEN LAYS ITS EGGS IN THE SHAFT *AND SEALS THE TUNNEL BY USING THE DIRT TURRET AS A PLUG*

126

THE DUKE d'EPERNON (1554-1642) FRENCH INFANTRY COMMANDER ALWAYS FAINTED AT THE SIGHT OF A YOUNG RABBIT

HE WAS NOT AFFECTED BY FULL-GROWN RABBITS

THE MOST INGENIOUS RESCUE IN HISTORY!

QUEEN SSU CHEI of Shansi, China, AFTER HER HUSBAND, KING TOBA-I-LU, HAD BEEN ASSASSINATED BY A MOB IN 316, SAVED HER INFANT SON *BY STRAPPING HIM TO HER LEG AND WALKING 12 MILES TO SAFETY WITH THE CHILD HIDDEN IN HER BAGGY TROUSERS!* ALTHOUGH ONLY ONE YEAR OF AGE, THE INFANT NEVER MADE A SOUND DURING THE ENTIRE JOURNEY

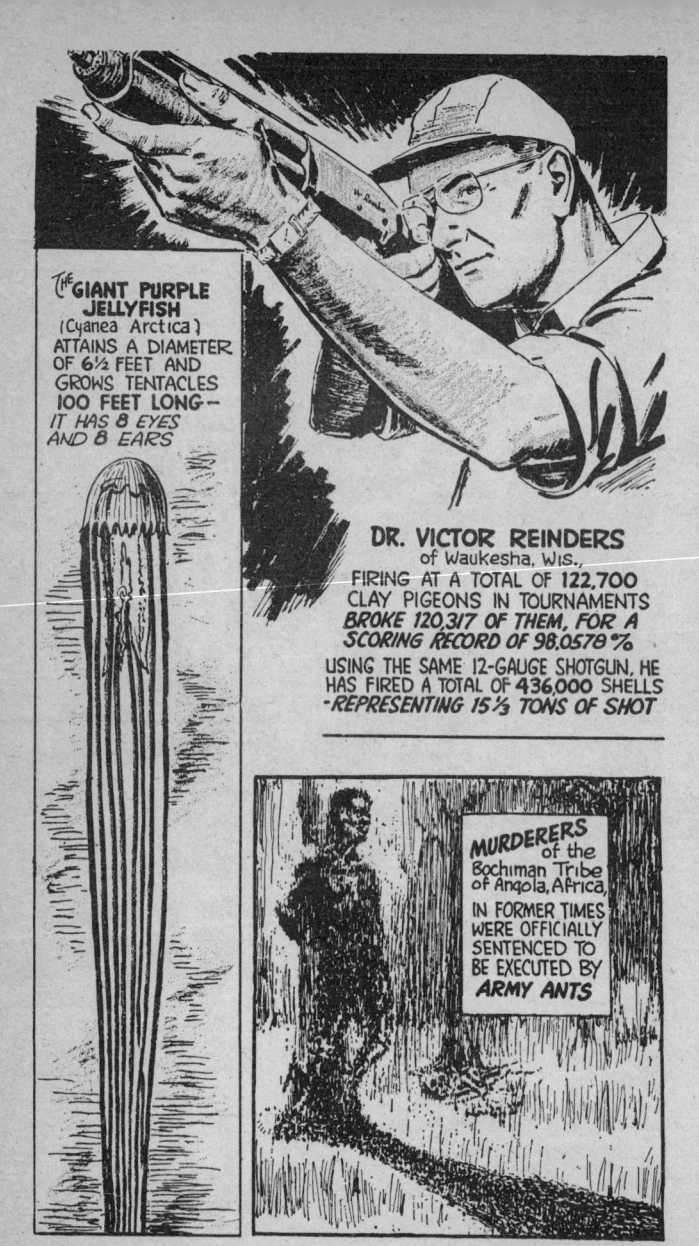

THE GIANT PURPLE JELLYFISH (Cyanea Arctica) ATTAINS A DIAMETER OF 6½ FEET AND GROWS TENTACLES **100 FEET LONG** — IT HAS 8 EYES AND 8 EARS

DR. VICTOR REINDERS of Waukesha, Wis., FIRING AT A TOTAL OF 122,700 CLAY PIGEONS IN TOURNAMENTS **BROKE 120,317 OF THEM, FOR A SCORING RECORD OF 98.0578%**

USING THE SAME 12-GAUGE SHOTGUN, HE HAS FIRED A TOTAL OF **436,000 SHELLS** — *REPRESENTING 15⅓ TONS OF SHOT*

MURDERERS of the Bochiman Tribe of Angola, Africa, IN FORMER TIMES WERE OFFICIALLY SENTENCED TO BE EXECUTED BY **ARMY ANTS**

LIGHT BULB WHICH HAS BURNED *EVERY NIGHT FOR 42 YEARS*
Owned by Mrs. T. Pascal,
New Haven, Conn.

A **FRENCH SCUBA DIVER**
EQUIPPED WITH FLIPPERS
AND AN AIR CYLINDER
*DEPICTED IN A PRINT
MADE 300 YEARS AGO*

GLACIERS
ARE THE ONLY NATURAL PHENOMENA *CAPABLE OF MOVING FORWARD AND BACKWARD AT THE SAME TIME*

BATTLE SHIELDS
USED BY
Natives of
Port Moresby,
New Guinea,
ARE MADE ONLY OF ROPE VINES AND THICK STEMS

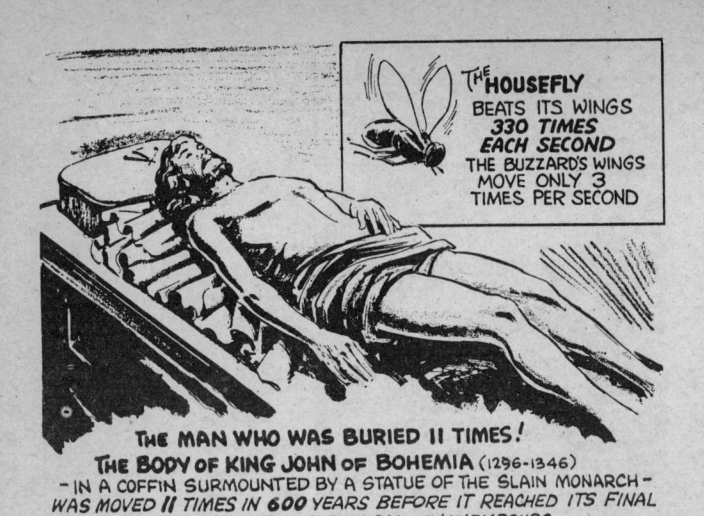

THE HOUSEFLY BEATS ITS WINGS **330 TIMES EACH SECOND**
THE BUZZARD'S WINGS MOVE ONLY 3 TIMES PER SECOND

THE MAN WHO WAS BURIED 11 TIMES!
THE BODY OF KING JOHN OF BOHEMIA (1296-1346)
– IN A COFFIN SURMOUNTED BY A STATUE OF THE SLAIN MONARCH –
WAS MOVED 11 TIMES IN 600 YEARS BEFORE IT REACHED ITS FINAL RESTING PLACE IN THE CATHEDRAL OF LUXEMBOURG

ARTHUR BENTON CRICKENBERGER of Bedford, Virginia, WAS GIVEN HIS NAME AS AN ALPHABETICAL PROGRESSION AS WERE HIS 6 BROTHERS:
CLINTON DEWITT
EARL FLOYD
GEORGE HERMAN
IRA JETHRO
KENNEY LUTHER and
MINOR NEWTON

THE ROCK MONASTERY OF ALADSHA
near Varna, Bulgaria
IT WAS CARVED OUT OF SOLID STONE

THE BAPTISTRY of the Cathedral of Ravenna, Italy, SERVED NEARLY 1,500 YEARS AGO *AS A ROMAN BATH*

AMOS WILSON (1781-1821) of Lebanon, Pa., SPENT THE LAST 19 YEARS OF HIS LIFE AS A CAVE-DWELLING HERMIT AFTER HIS SISTER WAS HANGED BECAUSE HE DELIVERED HER PARDON *2 MINUTES TOO LATE!*

HERE LIES
MARY BROOKS
WHO DIED IN 1736
AGED 11
SHE WAS VERY
EXCELLENT FOR
READING AND
SOBERNESS

Epitaph in the Hill Burying Ground, Concord, Mass.

The REV. **GUILLAUME SOUQUET de LATOUR** (1768-1850) Curate of St. Thomas Aquinas Parish, in Paris, France, TO GIVE HIMSELF MORE TIME TO STUDY LANGUAGES SLEPT ONLY 4 HOURS A NIGHT FOR THE LAST 40 YEARS OF HIS LIFE— *HE MASTERED 40 MODERN AND ANCIENT LANGUAGES*

IVAN MIHAILOV
Macedonian revolutionary
KILLED HIS GOOD FRIEND, ALEKSANDAR PROTOGEROV, A BULGARIAN GENERAL, IN SOFIA, BUT WAS RELEASED WHEN HE EXPLAINED TO POLICE:
"IF I HADN'T, YOU WOULD BE ASKING HIM NOW WHY HE KILLED ME"

THE KARAGAN
DANCED IN SOUTHERN INDIA, REQUIRES A GIRL TO GYRATE FOR HOURS WITH *A COPPER FLOWERPOT BALANCED ON HER HEAD*

NEWLYWEDS
in the village of Pont Melvez, France, ON THE FIRST MONDAY AFTER EASTER SUNDAY, WERE REQUIRED TO JUMP INTO THE RIVER LEGUER *3 TIMES IN A ROW - FULLY CLOTHED*

The PAPER NEST
of the Brazilian wasp *LOOKS AND SWINGS LIKE A JAPANESE LANTERN* - ACTUALLY IT IS A MINIATURE SKYSCRAPER, COMPRISING 20 OR MORE STORIES

THE BARON de FABVIER
(1782-1855)
WAS A GENERAL IN THE FRENCH ARMY

A GENERAL IN THE DANISH ARMY

A COLONEL IN THE GREEK ARMY

A MAJOR IN THE ARMY OF POLAND

A CAPTAIN IN THE TURKISH ARMY

AND A CAPTAIN IN THE ARMY OF PERSIA

THE RAGHUNATH TEMPLE in Jammu, India, WAS BUILT WITH 330,000,000 BRICKS - ONE FOR EACH INHABITANT OF INDIA AT THE TIME

PILGRIMS CIRCLE THE TEMPLE IN THE BELIEF THAT EACH TURN IS EQUIVALENT TO VISITING EVERY SACRED SPOT IN INDIA

THE SILKY A FOWL WITH WHITE BUSHY FEATHERS *HAS JET BLACK SKIN*

A **Monkey** in France WAS TRAINED BY THIEVES *AS A HOUSEBREAKER* IT WAS FINALLY CAPTURED AS THE RESULT OF A FINGERPRINT IT LEFT ON A WINDOWSILL

A **GLASS BALL** IN A FOUNTAIN IN A PRIVATE GARDEN IN MARSEILLES, FRANCE, WAS KEPT SUSPENDED IN EXACTLY THE SAME POSITION *BY 9 JETS OF WATER FOR A PERIOD OF 101 YEARS* (1615-1716)

SIR **PETER** LELY (1618-1680) BECAUSE A RIVAL ARTIST COMPLETED A PAINTING OF KING CHARLES II of England BEFORE SIR PETER FINISHED HIS PORTRAIT *WAS SO MORTIFIED THAT HE DIED*

THE **ASTROLOGER WHO PREDICTED HIS OWN DOOM!**

DAVID FABRICIUS (1546-1617) German astronomer and astrologer *PREDICTED IN 1607 THAT MAY 7, 1617 WOULD BE HIS FATAL DAY*

ON THAT DAY HE STAYED HOME WITH THE DOORS LOCKED, BUT AT MIDNIGHT HE EMERGED TO WALK IN HIS GARDEN *-AND A MANIAC SPLIT FABRICIUS' SKULL WITH A PITCHFORK*

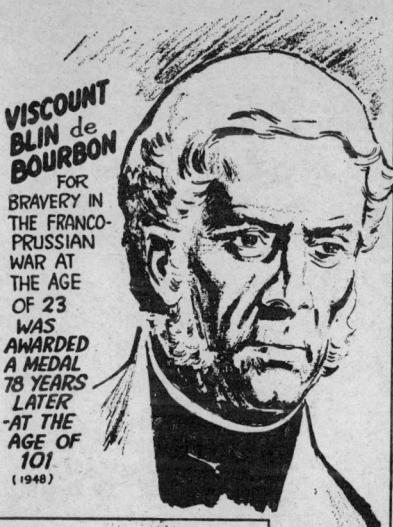

VISCOUNT BLIN de BOURBON FOR BRAVERY IN THE FRANCO-PRUSSIAN WAR AT THE AGE OF 23 *WAS AWARDED A MEDAL 78 YEARS LATER -AT THE AGE OF 101* (1948)

A **MONUMENT** TO THE WHALING INDUSTRY ERECTED IN FRONT OF THE CATHEDRAL IN PORT STANLEY, the Falkland Islands, *WAS MADE FROM THE JAWBONES OF WHALES*

I DON'T KNOW HOW TO DIE

Epitaph OF LIZZIE ANGEL WHO DIED IN 1932 AT THE AGE OF 83 Forest Hill Cemetery, East Derry, N.H.

The **PICTURE OF HEALTH**
ALBRECHT DÜRER (1471-1528) famed German painter ALWAYS TOO BUSY TO VISIT HIS DOCTOR, SENT HIS PHYSICIAN A SKETCH OF HIMSELF WHENEVER HE WAS ILL -WITH A FINGER POINTING TO THE SPOT WHERE HE FELT PAIN

THE SWORD AND HAT
OF COUNT EWALD von HERTZBERG, PRUSSIAN MINISTER OF FOREIGN AFFAIRS UNTIL HIS DEATH IN 1795, HAVE RESTED UNDISTURBED ON HIS COFFIN in the Church of Britz, Germany, *FOR 171 YEARS AND DESPITE THE LOOTING OF 2 WORLD WARS*

FIELD MARSHAL ABRAHAM de FABERT
(1599-1662) of France
AWARE THAT DEATH WAS NEAR CLIMBED OUT OF BED, DRESSED WITHOUT AID, KNEELED IN PRAYER -AND *DIED ON HIS KNEES*

CHINESE EMPERORS
for a period of 141 years ACKNOWLEDGED DEPENDENCE UPON THEIR SUBJECTS - *BY BEING CROWNED ON A BLANKET - HELD ALOFT BY A GROUP OF THEIR PEOPLE* (1227-1368)

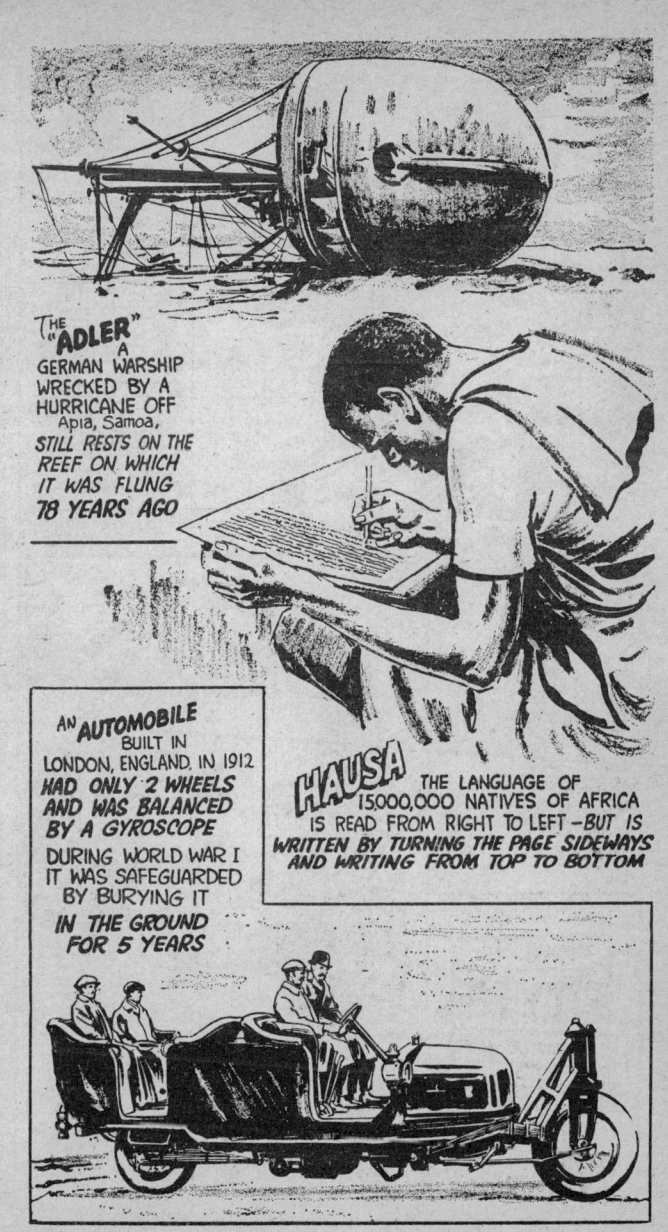

The "ADLER"
A GERMAN WARSHIP WRECKED BY A HURRICANE OFF Apia, Samoa, *STILL RESTS ON THE REEF ON WHICH IT WAS FLUNG 78 YEARS AGO*

AN **AUTOMOBILE** BUILT IN LONDON, ENGLAND, IN 1912 *HAD ONLY 2 WHEELS AND WAS BALANCED BY A GYROSCOPE*

DURING WORLD WAR I IT WAS SAFEGUARDED BY BURYING IT *IN THE GROUND FOR 5 YEARS*

HAUSA THE LANGUAGE OF 15,000,000 NATIVES OF AFRICA IS READ FROM RIGHT TO LEFT — BUT IS *WRITTEN BY TURNING THE PAGE SIDEWAYS AND WRITING FROM TOP TO BOTTOM*

THE TUBULAR NEST
BUILT BY THE SALVIN'S SWIFT, of Guatemala, IS CONSTRUCTED ENTIRELY OF SEEDS GLUED TOGETHER WITH SALIVA - AND HAS A FALSE ENTRANCE TO FOOL PREDATORS THAT MIGHT TRY TO REACH THE BIRD'S EGGS

THE MOST BINDING OATH in ancient Rome WAS SWORN OVER THE BODY OF A SLAVE *EXPRESSLY MURDERED FOR THE CEREMONY*

SIGN OUTSIDE PITY ME, A TOWN IN DURHAMSHIRE, ENGLAND

DURHAM 2½M
PITY ME
NEWCASTLE 12½M

JUDGE THOMAS LEONARD (1641-1713) of the Court of Common Pleas of Bristol County, Mass., HAD A SON, 2 GRANDSONS, A GREAT-GRANDSON AND 3 NEPHEWS - ALL OF WHOM SERVED AS JUDGES IN THE SAME COURT

A **GAMBLER'S BELT** WORN IN THE OLD WEST HELD **3** DOUBLE-ACTION REVOLVERS – WHICH COULD BE FIRED SIMULTANEOUSLY BY SQUEEZING ONE TRIGGER

THE **SPIRE** of the Church of the Minorites, in Vienna, Austria, WAS KNOCKED OFF BY A TURKISH ARTILLERY SHELL IN 1683 AND THE CHURCH HAS REMAINED IN THAT CONDITION AS A MEMORIAL *FOR 284 YEARS*

THE **STRANGEST** HYPOCHONDRIAC IN HISTORY
BARON OSKAR von REDWITZ
(1823-1891)
the German poet
FOR THE LAST 28 YEARS OF HIS LIFE COMPLAINED OF A NEW ILLNESS EVERY DAY – DESCRIBING MORE THAN 10,000 AILMENTS
EACH OF THEM UNKNOWN TO MEDICAL SCIENCE!

THE **SPADE FISH** CAN CHANGE ITS COLOR INSTANTANEOUSLY *AND APPEAR BLACK, WHITE OR BLACK AND WHITE*

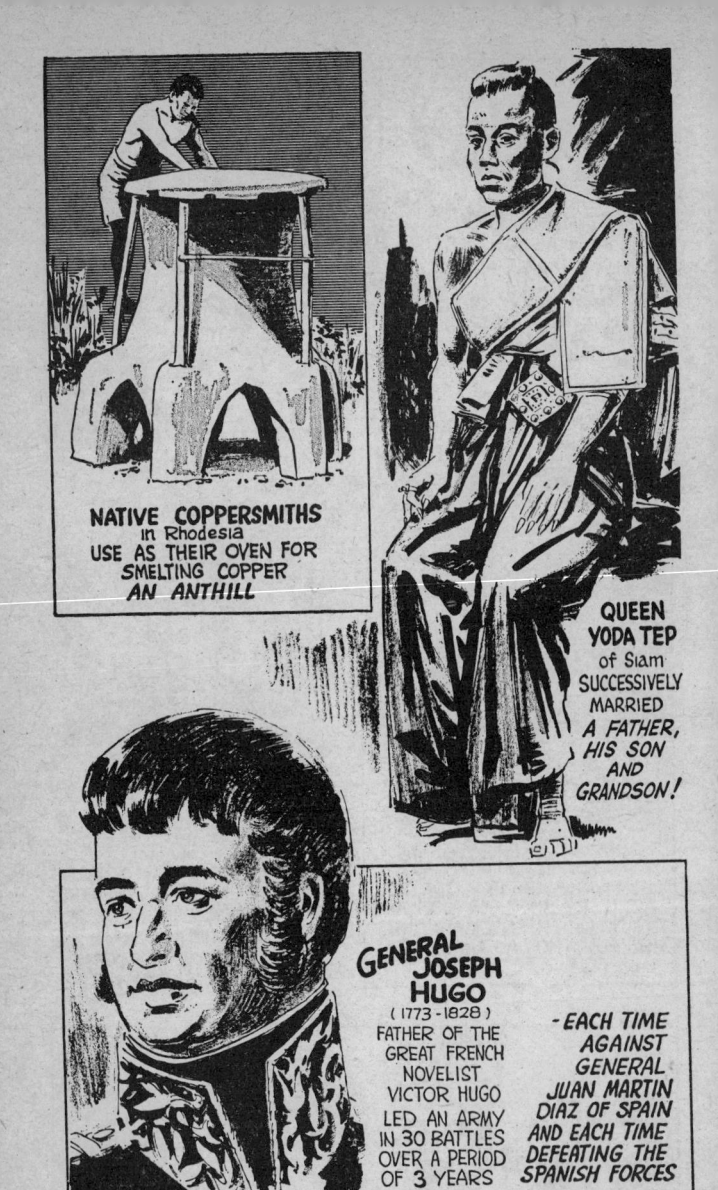

NATIVE COPPERSMITHS in Rhodesia USE AS THEIR OVEN FOR SMELTING COPPER *AN ANTHILL*

QUEEN YODA TEP of Siam SUCCESSIVELY MARRIED *A FATHER, HIS SON AND GRANDSON!*

GENERAL JOSEPH HUGO (1773-1828) FATHER OF THE GREAT FRENCH NOVELIST VICTOR HUGO LED AN ARMY IN 30 BATTLES OVER A PERIOD OF 3 YEARS — *EACH TIME AGAINST GENERAL JUAN MARTIN DIAZ OF SPAIN AND EACH TIME DEFEATING THE SPANISH FORCES*

PALLAS A SLAVE FREED BY EMPEROR CLAUDIUS of Rome, HAVING SUGGESTED THE EMPEROR'S MARRIAGE TO AGRIPPINA, WAS OFFERED A MARRIAGE BROKER'S FEE OF $645,000 BY THE ROMAN SENATE —BUT REFUSED IT ON THE GROUND THAT ALL MARRIAGES ARE *MADE IN HEAVEN*

THE **TWO-IN-ONE TOWER** THE BELFRY OF THE ABBEY OF SAINT MERCURIALE, in Forlì, Italy, BUILT IN 1180, IS PROTECTED BY BEING SHIELDED WITHIN ANOTHER TOWER THAT IS ITS *EXACT REPLICA*

FATHER DOMINIKUS PAMLER (1868-1955) WAS ORGANIST OF THE CHURCH OF MARIENSTATT, GERMANY, *FOR 65 YEARS*

POTATO DUCK

FERDINANDO PAER (1771-1839) of Parma, Italy, COMPOSED A SUCCESSFUL GRAND OPERA AT THE AGE OF **16**

The **BOW TREE** Pretoria, S. Africa
IT IS ROOTED AT BOTH ENDS

BEETLE MITE'S LARVA MOULTS ITS SKIN FREQUENTLY -BUT RETAINS EACH MOULT ON ITS BACK TO FORM A MEDALLION OF DAZZLING COLOR

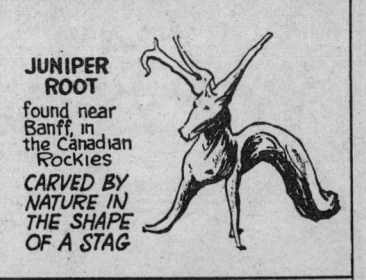

JUNIPER ROOT found near Banff, in the Canadian Rockies *CARVED BY NATURE IN THE SHAPE OF A STAG*

142

THE MONSTER OF MOROCCO

IBRAHIM II
WHO RULED MOROCCO AND SICILY FROM 875 TO 902, AS PUNISHMENT FOR A REBELLION IN BACOUSTA, MOROCCO, KILLED EACH OF ITS 500 INHABITANTS WITH HIS OWN HANDS —AND MURDERED 8 OF HIS BROTHERS AND ALL 16 OF HIS OWN DAUGHTERS

THE GATE
to the town of Moudon, Switzerland, IS LOCATED IN THE BASE OF *A CHURCH BELFRY*

THE AMAZING MOUNTAIN MOTHER OF ITALY

MAGDALENA VENTURA of the Abruzzi Mountains, AFTER HAVING BECOME THE MOTHER OF 3 CHILDREN *GREW A MOUSTACHE AND FLOWING BEARD AT THE AGE OF 32*

SHE THEN MARRIED AGAIN AND HAD FOUR MORE CHILDREN— *THE LAST WHEN SHE WAS 52*

THE CORPSE THAT WAS SENT TO THE GUILLOTINE

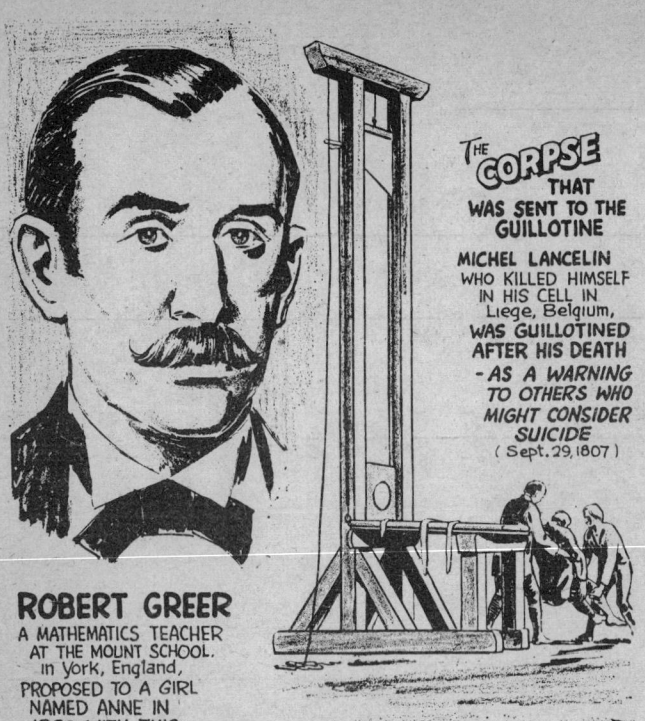

MICHEL LANCELIN WHO KILLED HIMSELF IN HIS CELL IN Liege, Belgium, WAS GUILLOTINED AFTER HIS DEATH - AS A WARNING TO OTHERS WHO MIGHT CONSIDER SUICIDE (Sept. 29, 1807)

ROBERT GREER

A MATHEMATICS TEACHER AT THE MOUNT SCHOOL in York, England, PROPOSED TO A GIRL NAMED ANNE IN 1880 WITH THIS MATHEMATICAL FORMULA:

IF $R = 1/2$ AND $A = 1/2$
THEN $R + A = 1$
BUT $R - A =$ NOTHING AT ALL

HER ANSWER "LET IT BE R+A"

ALARM CLOCK

OWNED BY JOHN S. BOWMAN, of Winter Park, Fla., HAS BEEN KEEPING PERFECT TIME FOR **336 YEARS**

BEAUTIFUL PAINTINGS

WERE MADE IN THE LATE 19th CENTURY BY P. FLORENTIN, OF PARIS, FRANCE, *ENTIRELY FROM HUMAN HAIR*

DR. THOMAS ARNOLD (1795-1842) THE ENGLISH EDUCATOR, REQUESTED AS HIS REWARD FOR SCHOLARSHIP A 24-VOLUME EDITION OF "THE HISTORY OF ENGLAND" *WHEN HE WAS 3 YEARS OF AGE*

FUNERAL PROCESSIONS in the Greek Islands ARE PRECEDED BY A PALLBEARER *CARRYING THE LID OF THE COFFIN* — THE PRACTICE ORIGINATED TO GIVE THE DECEASED A LAST LOOK AT THE WORLD FROM AN UNCOVERED COFFIN

THE MONARCH WHO NEVER LOST HIS TEMPER

EMPEROR NERVA, who ruled Rome from 96 to 98 AD, WHEN HE LEARNED OF A PLOT AGAINST HIS LIFE, ALWAYS INVITED ITS LEADER TO HIS SIDE, CHATTED CORDIALLY FOR A TIME, THEN TACTFULLY WAKNED THAT THE CONSPIRACY HAD BEEN EXPOSED BY ASKING:
"HAVE YOU SHARPENED YOUR DAGGER?"

NICCOLO PAGANINI (1784-1840) THE FAMED VIOLINIST HAD FINGERS WITH A SPAN OF 18 INCHES

"JINGLE ALL THE WAY" JINGLING LANE in Kirkby Longsdale, England, IS SO NAMED BECAUSE EVERY STEP UPON IT PRODUCES A SOUND EXACTLY *LIKE THE JINGLING OF A BELL*

THE LARGEST CIGARS IN THE WORLD 2 FEET, 8¼ INCHES LONG, ARE MADE IN ANDORRA - ONE OF THE SMALLEST COUNTRIES IN THE WORLD

A STONE found near Kincardine, Ontario, HAS THE NATURAL OUTLINE OF A *GIRL'S HEAD*

THE BATTLE THAT WAS WON WITH BUTTER!

MICHAEL de RUYTER (1607-1676) COMMANDER OF A DUTCH SHIP CARRYING A CARGO OF BUTTER *SAVED HIS VESSEL FROM FRENCH PIRATES BY GREASING THE DECKS, SIDES AND RIGGING WITH BUTTER*

THE **PET DOG** of LIEUT. LOUIS PFIEFF, of Chicago, Ill., WHO WAS SLAIN IN THE BATTLE OF SHILOH ON APRIL 7, 1862, KEPT A VIGIL BESIDE HIS GRAVE FOR 12 DAYS —AND FINALLY LED THE LIEUTENANT'S WIDOW TO THE UNMARKED GRAVE

DR. FRANCISCO VALLÉS

WAS MADE CHIEF PHYSICIAN TO KING PHILIP II OF SPAIN AND GIVEN THE OFFICIAL TITLE OF "DIVINE DOCTOR" *BECAUSE HE CURED THE MONARCH'S RHEUMATISM BY PRESCRIBING A FOOTBATH IN WARM WATER* (1572)

THE FIRST FLYING SAUCER

A *RING-SHAPED MONOPLANE* FLOWN BY TILGHMAN RICHARDS AND CEDRIC LEE, OF ENGLAND, *53 YEARS AGO*

A STONE IDOL
at the mouth of the Klamath River, Del Norte County, Calif.,
CARVED OUT OF THE ROCK BY NATURE WAS PRAYED TO BY INDIAN FISHERMEN *TO ASSURE THEIR SAFETY AND A GOOD CATCH*

PHILIPPE de SAVOIE
(1490-1533)
WAS NAMED BISHOP OF GENEVA, SWITZERLAND, AT THE AGE OF 5

THE WHEATEAR IS THE ONLY AMERICAN LAND BIRD THAT REGULARLY *MIGRATES BETWEEN NORTH AMERICA AND AFRICA*

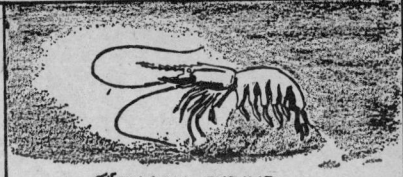

THE PELAGIC SHRIMP LIGHTS ITS WAY THROUGH THE OCEAN DEPTHS BY SURROUNDING ITSELF WITH *A HIGHLY LUMINOUS CLOUD*

AUSTRALIAN ABORIGINES of the Melville and Bathurst Islands AT THE BURIAL OF FELLOW TRIBESMEN *DANCE ON A BLAZING FIRE UNTIL THE HAIR HAS BEEN SINGED OFF THEIR BARE LEGS AND ARMS*

CONSTRUCTION of the Church of Beasain, Spain, WAS HALTED ON APRIL 26, 1665, BECAUSE NO MORE STONE WAS AVAILABLE IN THE AREA - AND THE CONGREGATION HAD NO FUNDS TO CART IN THE NEEDED ROCK *THAT VERY DAY A TREMENDOUS EARTHQUAKE SPLIT IN TWO AN ENTIRE MOUNTAIN-MAKING AVAILABLE ENOUGH STONE TO COMPLETE THE EDIFICE!*

The STONE LAMP

CHIRAG TASH, A CRAG in Ferghana, Uzbekistan, SHINES WITH A SCINTILLATING LIGHT —EVEN WHEN THE MOON IS HIDDEN BY CLOUDS

MARSHAL BOURMONT

(1773-1846) of France, CONQUEROR OF ALGERIA, *CARRIED WITH HIM FOR 16 YEARS THE HEART OF HIS SON AMEDEE —KILLED IN THE BATTLE OF SIDI IBRAHIM*

2 BRITISH Q SHIPS CAPTAINED BY COMMANDER GORDON CAMPBELL IN WORLD WAR I, WERE VISITED HUNDREDS OF MILES AT SEA BY A THRUSH *WHICH FLEW INTO THE CAPTAIN'S CABIN*

COMMANDER CAMPBELL'S SHIPS SANK 3 GERMAN SUBMARINES —*EACH ONE ON THE DAY FOLLOWING A VISIT BY THE THRUSH*

THE **LEBONG RACE COURSE**
near Darjeeling, India,
IS LOCATED ATOP A
6,000-FOOT MOUNTAIN AND
IS ONLY 1,320 FEET LONG

THE STONE GIANT
A CLIFF OVERLOOKING THE LÜTSCHINE
RIVER, NEAR LAUTERBRUNNEN, SWITZERLAND,
*BEING SHAPED BY STORMS, FLOODS AND
ICE TO FORM THE OUTLINE OF
A GIANT'S FACE*

THE **COPPER BUTTERFLY**
IS A VICIOUS FIGHTER

TWIN BOYS
of the Hill Maria Tribe, India,
OFTEN WEAR A SINGLE DRESS
— SIMULTANEOUSLY

151

THE BAG WORM LIVES IN A HOUSE CONSTRUCTED BY A CATERPILLAR OF LEAF FRAGMENTS FASTENED TOGETHER WITH SILK

THE HUECHA RIVER near EL SOMONTANO, Spain, *NOW FLOWS UNDERGROUND BENEATH ITS OLD BONE-DRY BED*— ITS WATERS VANISHED FROM THE SURFACE WHEN AN ATTEMPT WAS MADE TO DIVERT THEM FOR AN IRRIGATION PROJECT

ANTOINE DU PRAT (1463-1535) Chancellor of France BECAME SO FAT THAT TO ENABLE HIM TO REACH HIS FOOD *A LARGE NOTCH WAS CUT OUT OF HIS DINING ROOM TABLE*

THE CROW ALTHOUGH BLACK ITSELF *IS TERRIFIED OF ANYTHING ELSE THAT IS BLACK*

THE RHINOCEROS IS THE ONLY MAMMAL THAT DOES NOT HAVE TO BLINK TO LUBRICATE ITS EYES— FROM TIME TO TIME IT PULLS ITS EYES BACK INTO THEIR SOCKETS-AND TWIRLS THEM AROUND

THE VINEGAR CHURCH
THE CHURCH of SAN ANTONIO TAUMATURGO in Trieste, Italy, WAS CONSTRUCTED IN 1840 DURING A SEVERE DROUGHT -SO ITS MORTAR WAS MIXED WITH VINEGAR

COUNTESS WALEWSKA
WIFE OF THE FRENCH AMBASSADOR TO LONDON (1848-1851) WAS SO ADMIRED BY THE BRITISH THAT WHENEVER SHE DROVE BY IN HER CARRIAGE *MEN TOSSED IN RINGS, TIE PINS AND OTHER JEWELRY*

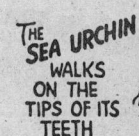

THE SEA URCHIN
WALKS ON THE TIPS OF ITS TEETH

Haworthia Pilifera
of Southern Rhodesia
A LILY THAT HALF-BURIES ITSELF IN THE GROUND AS A PROTECTION AGAINST THE COLD, GETS ITS SUNLIGHT THROUGH A COVERING *OF TRANSPARENT LEAVES*

THE OLDEST CHERRY TREE
A TREE STILL BEARING FRUIT ALTHOUGH IT IS 400 YEARS OLD- ITS BRANCHES HAVE TO BE PROPPED UP WITH POLES (Kyoto, Japan)

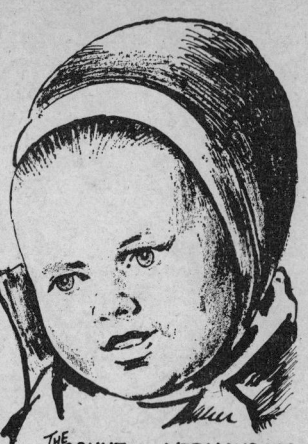

THE COUNT de VERMANDOIS WAS APPOINTED ADMIRAL OF THE FRENCH NAVY *WHEN HE WAS 2 YEARS OF AGE* (Nov. 12, 1669)

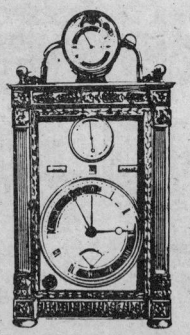

VALLEYS in the Libyan Desert, near Egypt, AS VIEWED FROM THE AIR *APPEAR IN THE SHAPE OF HUGE TREES*

THE **AUTOMATIC "WATCHMAKER"** A CLOCK CREATED BY ABRAHAM L. BREGUET, A FRENCH WATCHMAKER, IN 1795 *HAD THE POWER TO CORRECTLY ADJUST ANY WATCH THAT WAS LAID ATOP THE CLOCK FOR A SINGLE NIGHT*

JOSEPH SLOAN of Springfield, Mass., BOWLING IN A GAME OF CANDLEPINS, *SAW HIS BALL HOOK BETWEEN THE 1 AND 3 PINS WITHOUT TUMBLING A SINGLE PIN*

KING BAUDOUIN II of Jerusalem WAS CAPTURED BY THE SARACENS — AND SUCCEEDED IN ESCAPING — **11 TIMES!**
(1118-1131)

A PAIR OF ELK TRAINED BY JOHN O'BYRNE of Colorado Springs, Colo., **TO PULL A WAGON**
(1889-1891)

HEIDE
MUST REMAIN THE LARGEST MARKET PLACE IN GERMANY
IF A LARGER MARKET IS BUILT IN THE COUNTRY, HEIDE'S MARKET SQUARE MUST BE ENLARGED BY THE CONDEMNATION OF SURROUNDING BUILDINGS

HAILSTONES FELL IN FRANCE IN 1870 IN THE SHAPE OF *ARTICHOKES*

THE **NAME** OF A SMALL HILL IN THE HAWKE BAY AREA, NEW ZEALAND

TAUMATAWHAKA-TANGIHANGAKOAUAU-ATAMATEAPOKAI-WHENUAKITANATAHU

THIS IS REPUTED TO BE THE LONGEST PLACE NAME IN THE WORLD

THE SUMMIT WHERE TAMATEA POKAI WHENUA PLAYED HIS FLUTE TO HIS LOVED ONE

I WOULD NOT LIVE FOREVER

EPITAPH ON GRAVESTONE OF **TRIPHEA SHEPARD WHO DIED AT 99** Plainfield, Vt., Cemetery

---

ANTOINE CARNEVALE
an eccentric of Paris, France, OWNED 60 SUITS OF CLOTHES, *BUT EACH WAS CUT IN A STYLE THAT HAD BEEN OUT OF FASHION FOR 200 YEARS* — HE ATE NOTHING BUT POTATOES OR WHITE BEANS — ALTERNATING HIS SPARSE DIET EVERY 6 MONTHS

THE CEILING of the Forest Museum, in Gävle, Denmark, IS ORNAMENTED WITH *THE ENTIRE ROOT OF A GREAT TREE*

THE ROOT WAS REMOVED FROM THE GROUND UNDAMAGED BY FLUSHING THE SOIL WITH FIRE HOSES

LUKE JONES GARFIELD
of Athol, Mass.,
WAS CRUSHED BY A FALLING TREE
ON **JUNE 10, 1819,** AT THE AGE OF
11 YEARS, 9 MONTHS, 9 DAYS —
LUKE JONES, A COUSIN AFTER
WHOM HE WAS NAMED, HAD ALSO
*BEEN CRUSHED BY A FALLING TREE
ON A JUNE 10th AT THE AGE OF
11 YEARS, 9 MONTHS AND 9 DAYS*

THE **FRUIT** of India's Durian Tree IS DELICIOUS IN TASTE - *BUT SMELLS SO VILE AN EATER MUST HOLD HIS NOSE*

THE CITY MUSEUM
of Pola, Yugoslavia,
WAS ORIGINALLY THE TEMPLE
OF ROME AND AUGUSTUS
-DEDICATED 1953 YEARS AGO

AN IRON HORSE
ATOP AN OLD HOUSE
in Braunau, Austria,
COMMEMORATES A RACE
HORSE SLAUGHTERED FOR
FOOD DURING AN ENEMY
SIEGE IN 1743

THE
X
TREE
Majorca,
Spain

CEROPEGIA DICOTOMA
A DESERT PLANT
ONCE GREW LEAVES
-WHICH WASTED WATER
BY EVAPORATION
THROUGH THEIR
WIDE SURFACES
*NOW IT GROWS ONLY
THICK GREEN STEMS,
WHICH PERFORM THE
FUNCTIONS OF THE
LEAVES - AND
CONSERVE
WATER*

MARIA HUBER
(1695-1753) of Geneva, Switzerland,
CONVINCED THAT HER GREAT
BEAUTY WAS A SIN
*NEVER WAS WITHOUT HER BIBLE
DAY OR NIGHT FOR 41 YEARS*

FISH HOOK
USED BY
natives of
Oceania
*MADE OF
POLISHED
STONE*

THE HIGHEST TRACTION RAILROAD IN NORTH AMERICA
THE ARGENTINE CENTRAL R.R. of Colorado TRAVERSING A NARROW TRACK 16 MILES LONG CLIMBED TO THE PEAK OF MT. CLELLAN 13,644 FEET ABOVE SEA LEVEL
-WITH AN AVERAGE GRADE OF 5 1/3 %

THOMAS DIXON, Jr.
(1864-1946)
A PREACHER AND AUTHOR OF THE BOOK WHICH BECAME THE FAMOUS MOVIE, "A BIRTH OF A NATION," WAS ELECTED TO THE NORTH CAROLINA LEGISLATURE AT THE AGE OF 20
-A YEAR BEFORE HE WAS QUALIFIED TO VOTE

"THE DESERT ROSE" of the Great Plains of the Middle West ACTUALLY IS COMPOSED ENTIRELY OF SAND

RESIDENTS of Leyden, Holland, HAVE CELEBRATED THEIR VICTORY AGAINST THE SPANIARDS BY ENJOYING A FREE DISTRIBUTION OF WHITE HERRING AND BREAD THE ONLY FOOD AVAILABLE DURING THE SIEGE — ANNUALLY FOR 392 YEARS

UPPER LEAVES of the Monstera deliciosa, **A BRAZILIAN CLIMBING SHRUB, HAVE PERFORATIONS —TO ALLOW THE SUN TO REACH THE LOWER LEAVES**

WOMEN of the Ubangi-Chari Tribe, Africa, WEAR A HUGE BUSTLE OF GREEN LEAVES *TO ADVERTISE THAT THEY SEEK A HUSBAND*

THE **COUNTESS de MARBOEUF** WIFE OF A FRENCH ROYALIST GENERAL WAS SENT TO THE GUILLOTINE IN 1794 *BECAUSE SHE HAD PLANTED ALFALFA IN HER GARDEN* THE TRIBUNAL IGNORED THE FACT THAT SHE OWNED HORSES AND INSISTED SHE MUST HAVE RAISED ALFALFA TO FEED THE HORSES OF AN INVADING CAVALRY

THE "OSTRICH" BEETLE THE DARKLING BEETLE, WHEN THREATENED, STANDS ON ITS HEAD

THE **TOWER** of the town wall of Arbing, Austria, LATER SERVED AS THE TOWER OF A CASTLE AND *IN 1483 BECAME THE BELFRY OF THE TOWN'S CHURCH*

A **WITCH DOCTOR** of Tibet WHO INSISTS HIS HEALING POWERS ARE DERIVED FROM A CHARM CONSISTING OF THE HAIR FROM 200 PEOPLE *-100 OF THEM CORPSES*

THE HOLIDAY FAMILY
HENRY POZNER of San Diego, Calif., WAS MARRIED ON *LABOR DAY,* in 1940, HIS FATHER WAS BORN ON *CHRISTMAS DAY,* in 1857, HIS DAUGHTER JOANN WAS BORN ON *THANKSGIVING DAY,* 1942, HIS FIRST GRANDDAUGHTER WAS BORN ON *MEMORIAL DAY,* 1960, HIS FIRST GRANDSON WAS BORN ON *PEARL HARBOR DAY,* 1964, AND HIS SECOND GRANDDAUGHTER WAS BORN ON *VALENTINE'S DAY,* 1966

THE RESERVOIR PLANT
Bowela Volubilis, a So. African plant, LIES DORMANT FOR YEARS WHILE STORING UP THE SPARSE DESERT RAINFALL IN A BULB THAT SERVES AS ITS STORAGE TANK. WHEN THE TANK IS FULL OF WATER THE PLANT SENDS UP A STALK WHICH CONTINUES TO BLOSSOM UNTIL THE RESERVOIR IS EMPTY

KONRAD GOTTLIEB PFEFFEL
(1736-1809) of Colmar, France, FOUNDED AND RAN A FRENCH MILITARY ACADEMY *ALTHOUGH HE WAS TOTALLY BLIND*

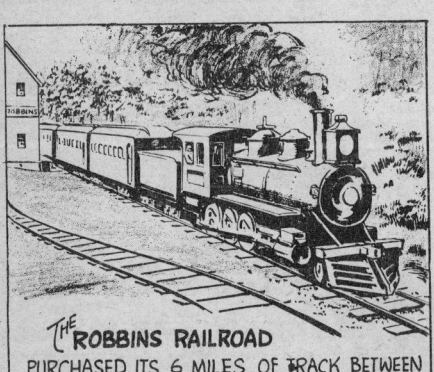

SIGNPOST
6D HANDLEY
OUTSIDE THE VILLAGE OF SIXPENNY HANDLEY, England

THE ROBBINS RAILROAD
PURCHASED ITS 6 MILES OF TRACK BETWEEN Rhinelander and Robbins Junction, Wis., in 1893 AT A PRICE OF $22 A TON, USED IT 48 YEARS *AND THEN SOLD IT AS SCRAP FOR $28 A TON*

A LEAF
OF THE CATHEDRAL BELLS PLANT WILL GROW A NEW PLANT *IF PINNED TO A CURTAIN*

THE THEATRE of ST. MARTIN'S GATE in Paris, France, WAS USED FOR 100 YEARS — YET IT WAS BUILT, DECORATED AND EQUIPPED IN 1781 *IN JUST 75 DAYS*

VERA PANINA GYPSY SINGER IN A NIGHT CLUB in St. Petersburg, Russia, JILTED BY A MEMBER OF THE CZAR'S GUARD SANG TO THE GUARDSMAN, "My heart is breaking" —THEN COMMITTED SUICIDE BY DRINKING POISON ON THE STAGE

HERE LIES THE BODY OF
JONATHAN TILTON
WHOSE FRIENDS REDUCED HIM
TO A SKELETON
THEY WRONGED HIM OUT
OF ALL HE HAD
AND NOW REJOICE THAT
HE IS DEAD

EPITAPH in Chilmark, Mass.

The TOPPIE
an African bird
BY SETTING UP AN INCESSANT CHATTER ALWAYS WARNS PASSERSBY OF THE PRESENCE OF *A CONCEALED SNAKE*

THE LEONBURG CASTLE
in Lana, Austria,
HAS BEEN OWNED BY THE SAME FAMILY FOR **700 YEARS**

EMPEROR CONSTANTINE VII
(905-959) of Byzantium
RULER OF THE EASTERN HALF OF THE ROMAN EMPIRE WAS SO BADLY IN NEED OF MONEY DURING THE FIRST 26 YEARS OF HIS REIGN THAT HE *MOONLIGHTED AS AN ARTIST*

164

THE GIRL WHO SACRIFICED ALL HER LOVED ONES TO SAVE A MAN SHE DID NOT KNOW!

Nilufer, daughter of a wealthy Greek named Belokoma HAVING LEARNED HER FATHER HAD INVITED SULTAN OSMAN OF TURKEY TO HER WEDDING TO AMBUSH AND SLAY HIM, **SENT A WARNING TO THE SULTAN**

OSMAN BROUGHT AN ARMY TO THE WEDDING AND KILLED EVERY MEMBER OF THE PARTY EXCEPT NILUFER - WHO SUBSEQUENTLY MARRIED THE SULTAN'S SON

THE MAIN ALTAR of the Church of Colloure, France, WAS CARVED BY JOSEPH SUNYER IN 3 YEARS FOR A FEE OF $600 - PLUS A TUNA FROM EVERY CATCH MADE IN THE AREA WHILE THE ALTAR WAS UNDER CONSTRUCTION

SUNYER COMPLETED THE PROJECT A YEAR AHEAD OF SCHEDULE BECAUSE HE BECAME TIRED OF EATING TUNA (1698-1701)

THE ERIE CANAL WAS RESPONSIBLE FOR CONSTRUCTION OF SCORES OF SIMILAR CANALS IN THE EARLY 19TH CENTURY U.S. - YET THE ERIE CANAL WAS THE ONLY ONE THAT OPERATED AT A PROFIT

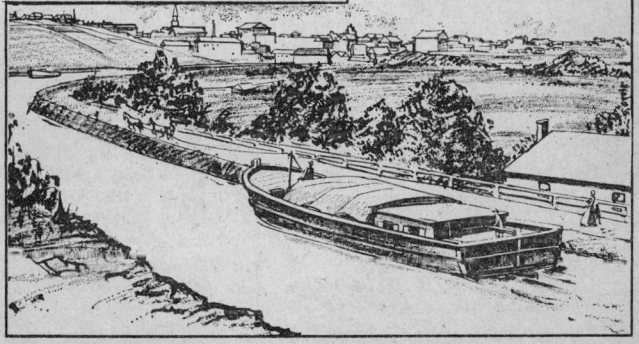

ALL VISITORS to the Imperial Castle, in Strasbourg, France, WHILE THE CITY WAS STILL PART OF GERMANY, HAD TO EXCHANGE THEIR SHOES FOR SLIPPERS WITH WAXED SOLES THE SLIPPERY SOLES CAUSED THEM TO GLIDE - *WHICH HELPED SHINE THE FLOORS*

THE **DUKE** OF **MONMOUTH** (1649-1685) SENTENCED TO DEATH FOR HIGH TREASON *TIPPED HIS EXECUTIONER 6 GUINEAS*

MARIE THERESE PARADIES (1759-1824) renowned pianist of Vienna, Austria, WAS STONE BLIND - *YET SHE COULD PLAY CARDS AND MERELY BY TOUCH RECOGNIZE THE FACE VALUE OF EVERY CARD*

A **HUMAN HAND** FOR CENTURIES HAS ADORNED THE GATE OF JUSTICE IN Granada, Spain. ITS FINGERS SYMBOLIZING THE 5 MOHAMMEDAN PRECEPTS - *FASTING, CHARITY, PRAYER, FAITH AND PILGRIMAGE*

THE GREAT HALL of Oakham Castle, in Rutland, England, IS ADORNED WITH ANCIENT HORSESHOES -EACH THE TRADITIONAL GIFT OF VISITING NOBILITY
THE OLDEST IS A HORSESHOE PRESENTED BY QUEEN ELIZABETH I ON A VISIT TO THE CASTLE 400 YEARS AGO

THE MOST FRAGILE JEWELRY IN THE WORLD
THE MEDICINE MAN of the Jivaro Indians of Ecuador WEARS LONG DANGLING EARRINGS *MADE FROM BEETLES' WINGS*
THEY ARE SO BRITTLE THEY NEVER LAST MORE THAN A SINGLE DAY

THE HOOP BARNACLE
WHICH BURROWS DEEPLY INTO THE SKIN OF WHALES HAS A HOOP-LIKE SHELL - AND AS ITS HEAD BURROWS DEEPER INTO THE WHALE *IT ADDS MORE AND MORE HOOPS TO ITS SHELL ON THE SURFACE*

THE RIVER BED of Pliches, in the Rouergue district of France, APPEARS TO HAVE BEEN PAVED BY SKILLED STONE MASONS -YET THE PATTERN OF VOLCANIC ROCK WAS CREATED ENTIRELY BY NATURE

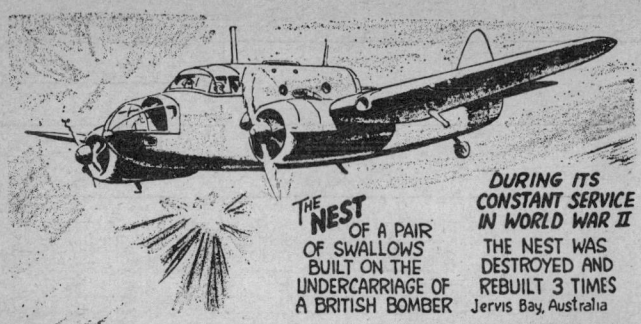

The NEST OF A PAIR OF SWALLOWS BUILT ON THE UNDERCARRIAGE OF A BRITISH BOMBER DURING ITS CONSTANT SERVICE IN WORLD WAR II THE NEST WAS DESTROYED AND REBUILT 3 TIMES Jervis Bay, Australia

The HOTEL des DOUANES in Nantes, France, WAS CONSTRUCTED BY GUILLAUME GROU, A WEALTHY SHIPBUILDER *SOLELY TO GIVE EMPLOYMENT TO WORKERS MADE IDLE BY THE DEVASTATING FROST OF 1770*

The NEST of LEAVES of the Phyllomedusa, a So. American frog, IS BUILT BY THE PARENTS' HOLDING THE EDGES OF SEVERAL LEAVES TOGETHER WITH THEIR FEET AND THEN POURING IN THE EGGS —THE STICKY SHELLS OF WHICH GLUE THE LEAVES INTO A PERMANENT CONE

WHISTLER WAS SO METICULOUS A PAINTER THAT OFTEN HE WOULD PAINT ALL DAY IN A WHITE SUIT —AND THEN GO OUT TO DINE THAT EVENING WEARING THE SAME IMMACULATE ATTIRE

THE MAORIS OF New Zealand SOUNDED ALARMS BY *HITTING THE HOLLOW TRUNKS OF DEAD TREES*

BIRDS OF A FEATHER
CATHERINE FINCH of York, England, SUCCESSIVELY MARRIED 4 HUSBANDS NAMED *CROWE, CRANE, HAWKE AND RAVEN*

A FREIGHT WAGON
OPERATED REGULARLY BETWEEN Tugela Mouth and Inyoni, in Zululand, S. Africa, *WAS PULLED BY 8 TRAINED ZEBRAS*

169

LOTUS PLANTS BLOOMING AT THE KENILWORTH AQUATIC GARDENS, Washington, D.C., GERMINATED FROM SEEDS FOUND IN MANCHURIA *THAT WERE 50,000 YEARS OLD*

JAMES BEALL of Russellville, Ky, WHO MARRIED 3 WOMEN *EACH TIME PICKED A WIFE NAMED SARAH*

A **MONUMENT** in Moron de la Frontera, Spain, ERECTED TO WARN OFF ENEMIES, FEATURES A **PLUCKED ROOSTER IN THE ACT OF CROWING**
THE MORAL: IF A PLUCKED ROOSTER CAN CROW, EVEN A LITTLE VILLAGE SHOULD NOT BE UNDERESTIMATED

A **BLACK STAR SAPPHIRE** THAT WAS CARVED INTO A LIKENESS OF PRESIDENT EISENHOWER, WEIGHED AS A ROUGH STONE — 2,097½ CARATS — THE CARVING REQUIRED 2 YEARS — AND DESTROYED 653½ CARATS

THE **ARROW-POISON BEETLE** of Africa IS SO CALLED BECAUSE ITS GRUBS YIELD THE VENOM BUSHMEN USE TO *MAKE LETHAL ARROWHEADS*

GRUB

Pride Goeth Before a Fall

THE TOMBSTONE OF MAYOR HANS STAININGER, of Braunau, Austria, DEPICTS HIM PROUDLY DISPLAYING HIS BEARD *WHICH WAS 8 FEET, 9 INCHES LONG*

HE DIED OF A BROKEN NECK, AFTER TRIPPING OVER IT

JAMES BERRY

BRITAIN'S OFFICIAL EXECUTIONER ALWAYS INTRODUCED HIMSELF TO THE CRIMINALS HE WAS ABOUT TO HANG BY GIVING THEM *HIS BUSINESS CARD*

THE SOUTH AMERICAN CATFISH DESPITE ITS NAME *GROWLS LIKE A DOG*

A *VIOLIN* CONSTRUCTED BY T.B. BUTLER, of Dallas, Texas, COULD PRODUCE RECOGNIZABLE TUNES *ALTHOUGH IT WAS MADE FROM A GOURD*

171

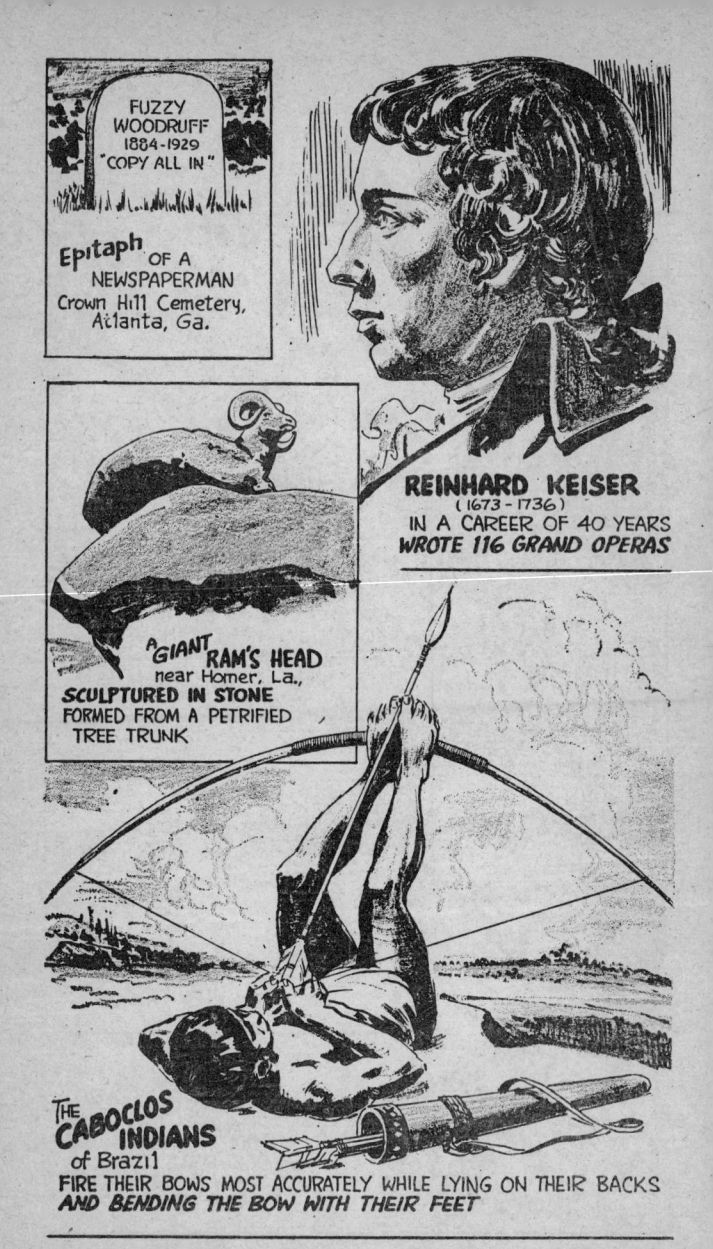

Epitaph OF A NEWSPAPERMAN
Crown Hill Cemetery, Atlanta, Ga.

FUZZY WOODRUFF
1884-1929
"COPY ALL IN"

REINHARD KEISER
(1673-1736)
IN A CAREER OF 40 YEARS
WROTE 116 GRAND OPERAS

A *GIANT* RAM'S HEAD near Homer, La., *SCULPTURED IN STONE* FORMED FROM A PETRIFIED TREE TRUNK

THE **CABOCLOS INDIANS** of Brazil
FIRE THEIR BOWS MOST ACCURATELY WHILE LYING ON THEIR BACKS *AND BENDING THE BOW WITH THEIR FEET*

172

VINEYARD WORKERS in the Canton of Valais, Switzerland, LABOR IN GROUPS OF FOUR WITH THREE DOING THE WORK —*AND THE FOURTH BEATING A DRUM*

A **YOUTH** in the Mundurucu Tribe, of Brazil, TO PROVE HIS FITNESS FOR MARRIAGE *IS BURIED NUDE FOR HOURS IN AN ANT HILL SWARMING WITH THE INSECTS*

SALMON ATTEMPTING TO LEAP UP THE WATERFALLS OF KILMORROCK, Scotland, FOR YEARS HAD TO AVOID A CAULDRON OF BOILING WATER POSITIONED UNDER THE FALLS BY RESIDENTS OF THE NEARBY CASTLE *WHO MADE A MEAL OF ANY SALMON THAT FELL INTO THE POT*

DOCUMENTS

GRANTING 4 LAND COMPANIES 35,000,000 ACRES OF GEORGIA FOR ONLY $500,000 WERE PUBLICLY BURNED BY THE 1796 STATE LEGISLATURE BY HARNESSING THE RAYS OF THE SUN WITH A BURNING GLASS —*ON THE THEORY THAT THE DEAL WAS SO FRAUDULENT HEAVEN ITSELF SHOULD WIPE IT OUT*

14 YEARS LATER THE SUPREME COURT RULED THE SALE VALID AND ORDERED GEORGIA TO PAY $5,000,000 IN COMPENSATION

JOHN WOODCOCK
ENGLISH SPORTSMAN
TO WIN A BET OF $10,185
COVERED 3,103 MILES ON HORSEBACK IN 29 DAYS - AVERAGING 107 MILES A DAY
May 4 to June 1, 1761

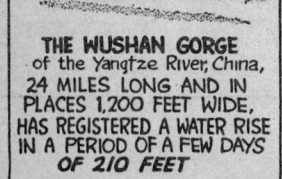

THE WUSHAN GORGE
of the Yangtze River, China, 24 MILES LONG AND IN PLACES 1,200 FEET WIDE, HAS REGISTERED A WATER RISE IN A PERIOD OF A FEW DAYS **OF 210 FEET**

THE MOPOKE
an Australian bush bird
WHEN SITTING ON A LIMB OF THE TI TREE *LOOKS LIKE A TREE BRANCH*

THE GARDENER ANT of the Amazon BUILDS NESTS OF MUD IN THE SHAPE OF A BALL AND TO HOLD IT TOGETHER PLANTS SEEDS — WHICH MAKE IT LOOK LIKE A MINIATURE *FLOWER GARDEN*

A **BRIDE** in Iran ALWAYS HAS A CLOTH SEWED ABOVE HER ON HER WEDDING-DAY — AS A *SEALING OFF OF ANY SLANDER AGAINST HER CHARACTER*

INFANTS IN THE CHAMA TRIBE OF PERU ARE MADE "BEAUTIFUL" BY BINDING THEM IN A WOODEN PRESS — *TO GIVE THEM A RECEDING FOREHEAD*

The **CHURCH** of **OUR LADY** in Guadalupe, Mexico, PEALS ITS CHURCH BELLS EVERY DAY *FROM MORNING TO NIGHT*

The **FIRST HARVESTER** A STONE DISCOVERED IN BELGIUM IN 1958 DEPICTS A HARVESTING MACHINE ON WHEELS *USED IN ANCIENT GAUL 1,900 YEARS AGO*

THE STRANGEST APTITUDE TEST IN HISTORY

JACQUES TESTU (1626-1706) a member of the French Academy IN AN ATTEMPT TO CONVINCE KING LOUIS XIV THAT HE WAS STILL QUALIFIED FOR EMPLOYMENT AT 80, DEMONSTRATED HIS CO-ORDINATION *BY POURING A PITCHER OF ICE WATER OVER HIS OWN HEAD - WITHOUT SPILLING A SINGLE DROP ON HIS CLOTHING*

MOUNT ATHOS Greece
IS THE SITE OF **40** MONASTERIES INHABITED BY SOME **7,000** MONKS, *BUT JUST A SINGLE NUNNERY — HOUSING ONLY ONE NUN*

LEE CLAFLIN
(1791-1871)
WAS A FOUNDER OF HOPKINSON, CLAFLIN AND BOSTON UNIVERSITIES, A TRUSTEE OF WILBRAHAM ACADEMY AND WESLEYAN UNIVERSITY, PRESIDENT-TRUSTEE OF THE CONCORD BIBLICAL INSTITUTE, *AND PRESIDENT OF THE BOARD OF GOVERNORS OF BOSTON THEOLOGICAL SEMINARY*

THE **BATH WHITE BUTTERFLY**
WAS NAMED IN ENGLAND IN 1702 *BECAUSE OF ITS RESEMBLANCE TO A PIECE OF EMBROIDERY CREATED IN BATH, ENGLAND*

A **TOMB** in the Mzab district of Algeria
HAS 2 SPIRES TO MARK THE GRAVE OF A MAN *BUT WOMEN'S GRAVES HAVE A 3RD SPIRE TO GIVE THEM A **FEELING OF SUPERIORITY***

THE **PRECIOUS WENTLETRAP**
ONCE SO RARE A SHELL THAT IT WAS EXTREMELY EXPENSIVE *NOW IS SURPASSED IN VALUE BY IMITATIONS OF IT FASHIONED BY A CHINESE ARTIST FROM RICE PASTE*

THE LARGEST BLOCK OF SALT IN THE WORLD

THE SALT MINE OF BARAHONA in the Dominican Republic CONSISTS OF A MOUNTAIN OF SALT 14 MILES LONG

THE MOST DAZZLING TEETH IN THE WORLD

GIRLS of the Kouroussa Tribe, Africa, CARRY A TOOTHBRUSH IN THEIR MOUTHS EVERY WAKING MOMENT *AND BRUSH THEIR TEETH EVERY HOUR*

KUANYAMA MAIDENS

of Ovamboland, Southwest Africa, ADVERTISE THEY ARE SEEKING A HUSBAND *BY SEWING A DECORATIVE WIG TO THEIR SCALP WITH NEEDLE AND THREAD*

WOMEN of Segovia, Spain, ONCE EACH YEAR, ON FEB. 5TH, DON MEDIEVAL COSTUMES -AND ONE OF THEM SERVES AS MAYOR

THE PAGANI THEATRE in Monterubbiano, Italy, WAS CONSTRUCTED IN 1862 ON THE FOUNDATION AND WALLS OF A PALACE THAT STOOD *UNFINISHED FOR 279 YEARS*

DONNA LYNN CAPONITI of Silver Spring, Md., WAS BORN AT 2:19 P.M. ON AUG. 2, 1966
HER FATHER, ALFRED, WAS BORN AT 2:19 P.M. ON AUG. 2, 1943

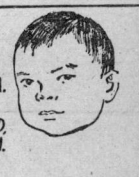

THE RIVER THAT MADE ITS OWN BRIDGE
THE **AGUANA RIVER** near Santander, Spain, HAS CARVED OUT OF A GREAT MASS OF ROCK *A BRIDGE NOW USED REGULARLY TO CROSS IT*

THE **OLD MISSION HOUSE** at Te Awamutu, N. Zealand, HAD WINDOW FRAMES *MADE FROM THE HOOPS OF OLD RUM CASKS* —

THE HOUSE CONTINUED TO EXUDE THE FRAGRANCE OF RUM FOR THE ENTIRE 40 YEARS OF ITS EXISTENCE

PIERRE DANIEL HUET
(1630 - 1721)
The Bishop of Avranches, France, MASTERED HEBREW BY READING THE OLD TESTAMENT IN THAT LANGUAGE 24 TIMES FROM *COVER TO COVER*

THE MEMORIAL TO A DREAM
THE PUBLIC FOUNTAIN in Schwerin, Germany, DEPICTS CIGAR DEALER JOHANNES MUHLENBURCH **AND 4 SEALS** — *HE SAW 4 SEALS IN A DREAM, CONSULTED A "DREAM BOOK," THEN BOUGHT A LOTTERY TICKET THAT WON HIM A FORTUNE*

AN OUTDOOR THEATRE
WAS CREATED ANNUALLY FOR YEARS NEAR PUCHHEIM, AUSTRIA, *BY LAYING PLANKS ACROSS HORIZONTAL LIMBS OF A TALL LINDEN TREE* 4 STAGES WERE SET UP TO MAKE A 4-STORY THEATRE ACCOMMODATING 140 ACTORS

KING WAJID ALI SHAH
of Oudh, India, DIVORCED 8 OF HIS WIVES ON THE SAME DAY BECAUSE A PROPHET DECLARED THAT A BIRTHMARK IN THE SHAPE OF A COILED SERPENT FORETOLD THE DEATH OF A MONARCH *ALL 8 WIVES WERE FOUND TO HAVE SUCH A BIRTHMARK*

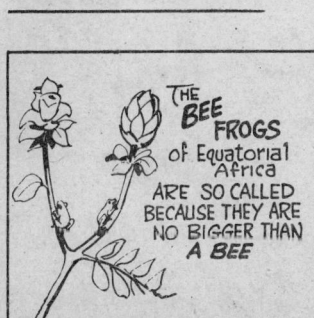

THE BEE FROGS of Equatorial Africa ARE SO CALLED BECAUSE THEY ARE NO BIGGER THAN *A BEE*

JAKOB PETER
SCHOOLMASTER of Elgg, Switzerland, from 1624 to 1671 *WAS SUCCEEDED IN THAT POST BY 10 DIRECT DESCENDANTS—* A MEMBER OF THE PETER FAMILY WAS A SCHOOLMASTER *FOR 164 SUCCESSIVE YEARS*

181

THE TOWER THAT WAS TRUE TO ITS PROPHECY

THE MOSQUE OF SULTAN HASSAN in Cairo WAS UNDER CONSTRUCTION IN 1359 WHEN A SOOTHSAYER WARNED THE SULTAN THAT THE SECOND MINARET HE COMPLETED WOULD CAUSE HIS DEATH

IN 1361 THAT MINARET CRASHED DOWN UPON AN ORPHANAGE AND KILLED 300 CHILDREN -- AND 33 DAYS LATER THE SULTAN DIED OF A BROKEN HEART

WILD GEESE of Osoyoos, Canada, INSTEAD OF NESTING ON THE GROUND, OCCUPIED THE TREE NESTS OF FISH HAWKS-- AS A RESULT THE GOSLINGS HAD TO BE *FLOWN TO THE GROUND EACH DAY ON THE BACKS OF THEIR MOTHERS*

ABORIGINES of arid Central Australia STARVED FOR SWEETS-- DIG UP THE NESTS OF HONEY ANTS AND EAT THE INSECTS LIKE CANDY

THE KAZAK KIRGHISIANS of Soviet Asia ARE SUCH EXPERT HORSEMEN THEY CAN SCOOP A CUP FILLED WITH MILK FROM THE GROUND AT FULL GALLOP -- AND THEN REPLACE IT WITHOUT SPILLING A DROP

RANNULF FLAMBARD WHO BUILT THE TOWER OF LONDON WAS THE FIRST MAN IMPRISONED IN IT - *BUT HIS FAMILIARITY WITH ITS ARCHITECTURE ENABLED HIM TO ESCAPE FROM IT*

WAR GALLEYS in medieval Europe NO MATTER HOW HEATED THE BATTLE ALWAYS STOPPED FIGHTING EACH NIGHT FOR PEACEFUL SLUMBER
A LARGE TENT WAS STRETCHED OVER THE SHIP AT NIGHT AND REMOVED THE NEXT MORNING - WHEN THE BATTLE WOULD RESUME

A **CHARM** designed by the painter HOLBEIN in the 16th century WAS BELIEVED PROTECTION FOR ITS WEARER AGAINST *HEART AND LIVER ILLS, POISON, HEAT BOILS, IMPRISONMENT, HEADACHES, BAD ADVICE, SORE EYES, WITCHCRAFT AND ENEMIES*

KING POMARE II (1781-1821) of Tahiti WHO BECAME A CHRISTIAN IN 1807 *TRANSLATED THE ENTIRE BIBLE INTO TAHITIAN*

THIS BRIDGE at Maidenhead, England, FOR 200 YEARS CHARGED TRAFFIC PASSING OVER IT ONE PENNY - BUT TRAFFIC PASSING UNDER IT PAID A *HALFPENNY MORE*

CLAUDE PERIER (1742-1801) FRENCH BANKER AND LEGISLATOR *HAD 5 SONS SERVING IN THE FRENCH PARLIAMENT SIMULTANEOUSLY*

THE PAGODA THAT HONORS A TREE on the River Min, near Fuchow, China
THE PAGODA WAS BUILT AS A TRIBUTE TO THE TREE THAT *MYSTERIOUSLY THRIVES ON AN ISLAND OF SOLID ROCK*

EAGLES CAN LOOK DIRECTLY INTO THE SUN WITHOUT BLINKING BECAUSE THEY HAVE *A THIRD EYELID*

BON VOYAGE ISLAND near Rio de Janeiro, Brazil, WAS GIVEN THAT NAME IN BRAZIL'S COLONIAL ERA BECAUSE EACH SHIP RETURNING TO PORTUGAL *RECEIVED THE INHABITANTS' TEARFUL GOODBYES FROM ATOP THE ISLAND'S CLIFFS*

THE ETRUSCAN SHREW ONLY 3 INCHES IN LENGTH *IS THE SMALLEST ADULT MAMMAL IN NATURE*

EMPEROR MING HUANG (716-756) PLAYED POLO ALL HIS ADULT LIFE — *BUT ALWAYS INSISTED THAT BOTH TEAMS BE MOUNTED ON MULES*

COLONEL THEODORE PEIN (1810-1893) WAS A DARING SOLDIER FOR 23 YEARS- YET *HE WAS AFRAID TO SIT IN A DENTIST'S CHAIR-* WHEN HE HAD TO HAVE A TOOTH PULLED, HE ALWAYS TIED A STRING FROM THE TOOTH TO A BOOK- AND THREW THE BOOK DOWN A STAIRWELL

The **ARACEAE**, A PLANT of French Guiana, ATTACHES ITSELF TO THE BRANCHES OF A TREE, BUT IT GETS ITS FOOD FROM THE AIR *AND SIPS ITS WATER THROUGH 70-FOOT-LONG TUBES WHICH IT LOWERS INTO THE SWAMPS*

The **DIGITS** IN THE LANGUAGE OF THE ANCIENT MAYAS of Central America WERE REPRESENTED BY DRAWINGS OF *19 DIFFERENT HUMAN HEADS*

The **MUSKOX** FIGHTING A WOLF, LEAPS HIGH INTO THE AIR TO LAND ON THE WOLF ON ITS BACK

THE **VERANDA**
of the CHION-IN TEMPLE,
in Kyoto, Japan,
IS SO CONSTRUCTED THAT
EACH HUMAN STEP CAUSES
ITS BOARDS TO SQUEAK WITH
*A SOUND RESEMBLING THE
SONG OF A NIGHTINGALE*

A **WATCH** CREATED FOR
THE DUKE OF PRASLIN IN 1785
GIVES THE TIME IN 5 DIFFERENT
ZONES, IS A PERPETUAL CALENDAR
AND A DEPENDABLE THERMOMETER
-*AND RINGS EACH MINUTE*

THE **CRAZED ELEPHANT THAT TOSSED
ITS KILLER TO SAFETY**

REGINALD MONTGOMERY
a government hunter
WHO HAD KILLED 197 ELEPHANTS
IN A PERIOD OF 3 YEARS
ONCE FIRED 3 BULLETS INTO
THE HEAD OF AN ELEPHANT
WITHOUT DROPPING IT-
*THE MADDENED TUSKER TOSSED
MONTGOMERY INTO A HIGH TREE
-WHERE HE REMAINED CONCEALED
UNTIL THE ANIMAL FINALLY DIED*

- 187

THE SQUIRTING CUCUMBER SHOOTS ITS SEED OVER AN AREA OF **30** FEET

THE KILLER WHO WAS HANGED 21 TIMES!
THE VISCOUNT OF NARBONNE WHO DIED IN THE BATTLE OF Verneuil, France, FOR HIS PART IN THE MURDER OF THE DUKE OF BOURGOGNE WAS EXHUMED FROM A MASS GRAVE AND CUT INTO 21 PIECES — *AND EACH PIECE OF HIS BODY WAS HANGED ON A DIFFERENT GALLOWS!*
August, 1424

THE GREAT LINDEN TREE
of Kunersdorf, Prussia,
SUPPORTED A HUGE PLATFORM HIGH IN ITS BRANCHES *ON WHICH THE ENTIRE VILLAGE ASSEMBLED FOR THE ANNUAL DANCE*

THE FREAK SHARK
A SHARK KILLED IN AUSTRALIA IN 1934 *MADE A MOANING SOUND AND SPAT WATER*

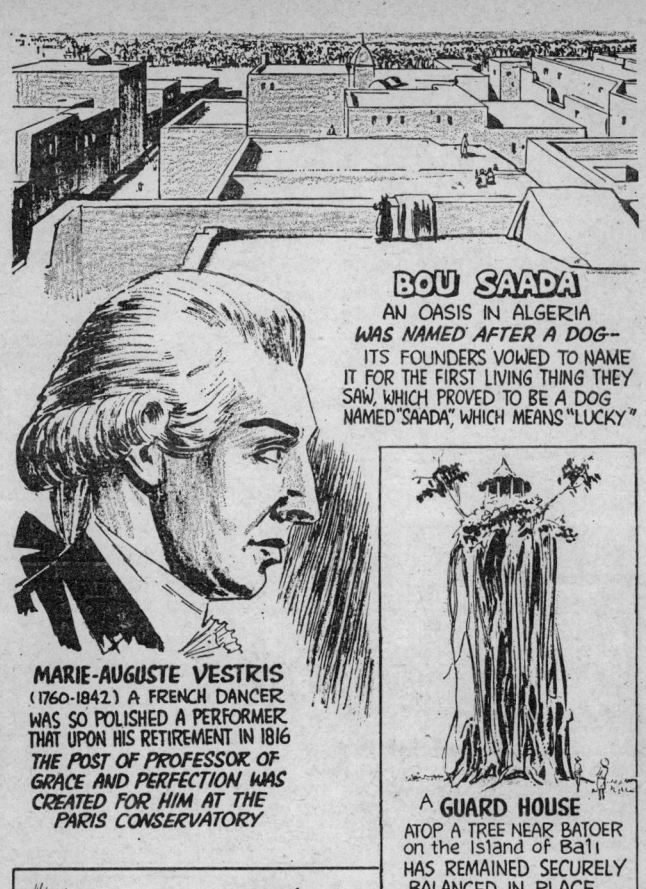

BOU SAADA
AN OASIS IN ALGERIA *WAS NAMED AFTER A DOG--* ITS FOUNDERS VOWED TO NAME IT FOR THE FIRST LIVING THING THEY SAW, WHICH PROVED TO BE A DOG NAMED "SAADA", WHICH MEANS "LUCKY"

MARIE-AUGUSTE VESTRIS (1760-1842) A FRENCH DANCER WAS SO POLISHED A PERFORMER THAT UPON HIS RETIREMENT IN 1816 *THE POST OF PROFESSOR OF GRACE AND PERFECTION WAS CREATED FOR HIM AT THE PARIS CONSERVATORY*

A **GUARD HOUSE** ATOP A TREE NEAR BATOER on the Island of Bali HAS REMAINED SECURELY BALANCED IN PLACE *ALTHOUGH THE TRUNK OF THE TREE HAS COMPLETELY DISINTEGRATED AND ONLY BRANCHES AND ROOTS SUPPORT THE STRUCTURE*

WOMEN of the Mzab district of Algeria MUST WEAR A HOOD THAT PERMITS THEM TO SEE THE OUTSIDE WORLD THROUGH *ONLY ONE EYE*

PATROLMEN **ROMEO** and **LOVE** SHARE THE SAME PATROL CAR IN WILDWOOD-BY-THE-SEA, N.J.

HOT DOGS

THE COUNTESS WILHELMINE (1709-1758) of Bayreuth, Germany, SISTER OF KING FREDERICK THE GREAT OF PRUSSIA, TO KEEP HER FEET WARM IN WINTER ALWAYS SLEPT WITH 7 DOGS *GROUPED AROUND HER FEET*

THE CASTLE OF EU in France, WAS OBTAINED FOR HIS SON, THE DUKE OF MAINE, BY KING LOUIS XIV BY CHARGING ITS OWNER, *THE DUKE OF LAUZUN, WITH TREASON AND SENTENCING HIM TO THE BASTILLE -THE DUKE WAS FREED WHEN HE SIGNED A DEED TO THE CASTLE*

HE LIVED
HE WEPT
HE SMILED
HE GROANED
AND DIED

Epitaph of SIDNEY ELLIS WHO DIED IN 1836 AT THE AGE OF 7 WEEKS Center Cemetery, Paxton, Mass.

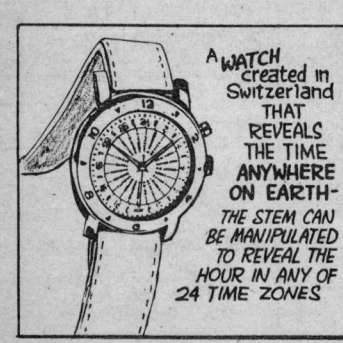

A **WATCH** created in Switzerland THAT REVEALS THE TIME ANYWHERE ON EARTH— *THE STEM CAN BE MANIPULATED TO REVEAL THE HOUR IN ANY OF 24 TIME ZONES*

THE GRAVE OF ROBIN HOOD near Kilkees, England, IS LOCATED ON THE SPOT *WHERE HIS LAST ARROW HIT THE EARTH*